# SALON MANAGEMENT GUIDE

*to*

# DOUBLE YOUR ~~SALE~~ PROFIT!

GUNJANN TANEJA

AF658009

DIAMOND BOOKS

www.diamondbooks.in

**Publisher** : **Diamond Pocket Books (P) Ltd.**
X-30, Okhla Industrial Area, Phase-II
New Delhi-110020

Phone : 011-40712200
E-mail : wecare@diamondbooks.in
Website : www.diamondbooks.in
Edition : 2025
Printed by : Repro India Ltd.
ISBN : 978-93-7122-605-9

**Salon Management Guide To Double Your ~~Sale~~ Profit**
**By - GUNJANN TANEJA**

# DEDICATED TO

They say making a decision is halfway to your destination. But it's easier said than done.

This book is dedicated to all those who chose the salon industry as their career.

To the brave tribe who shattered the myth that beauty was a fallback option for those who couldn't succeed academically.

To every individual who picked up a bag full of scissors, combs, brushes, and spatulas and said,
"Let's open a salon!
Let my name shine!
Let me make you confident and earn money along with blessings!"

This book is dedicated to you ….let the Tribe Grow!!!

# SPECIAL THANKS!!

This book is special to me—it's my hattrick! After publishing two books on Salon Management and Salon Retail Management, this is the third, it is a continuation of that journey.

Writing this book was a special journey. I took a break, escaped to the hills, and let the words flow. I truly believe that if you have the will and a story to tell, you should document it—for the generations to come.

While the first two books were intended for beginners, this book serves as an advanced guide on how to earn money and maximize profits in the salon industry.

My heartfelt thanks to Col Sanjay Sharma, who showed immense confidence in me and edited the book alongside the writing process. Thanks to his support, this mission was completed in less than a month!

I truly hope it adds extra feathers to the caps of salon owners everywhere and helps them achieve greater profits and success!!

# ABOUT THE BOOK

"Atithi Devo Bhava" means treat your guest like God. The same principle applies to your business too. Think of it as "Client Devo Bhava" — serve your client like God. Once this belief becomes part of your system, your entire approach to treating each walk-in will change.

You might be thinking, "She is not God, come on Gunjann!" But trust me, if I break it down, I can prove it in less than a minute. There are at least 10 salons with trained staff and attractive offers in your locality, yet she walks into yours. This is a test of your knowledge and skills — a divine test, if you will. If you satisfy her with both skill and knowledge, she rewards you with Dhan Lakshmi, bringing prosperity not only to you but also to those who depend on you. See, I love that smile!

Now imagine she walked into the salon next door. Would your day have gone the same way? Probably not. My personal secret to performing well in this field has always been my unwavering belief in this mindset. And this never failed.

I won't lie - I do come across difficult clients or those I may not agree with. But then again, who said pleasing God was ever easy? Or that God would always be pleased and grant your wish every time?

Take two minutes, close this book, and think about it. Picture a salon that smells great, has a positive aura, treats you with the highest level of respect, is honest in its words, cares for your smallest comfort and demands - wouldn't you want to keep going back there? Imagine the entire experience from walk-in to walk-out. If you find yourself smiling and feeling good, that's exactly the kind of atmosphere you need to recreate in your own salon.Do this, and your clients will never feel the need to look for a second option. Sure, clients are looking for good service within their budget - and almost every salon offers that. But what this book aims to cover is the extra X factor that silently turns a client into your forever client!

Post my two books on Salon Management and Salon Retail Management, this volume dives deeper into high-level strategies, including advanced marketing techniques, upscale service offerings, dynamic pricing models, staff productivity optimization, and leveraging technology for business growth. It is designed for salon owners and professionals who are ready to elevate their business and significantly enhance their bottom line.Whether you're looking to expand your brand, increase client retention, or explore new revenue streams, this book provides the expert insights and actionable steps you need to thrive in a competitive market.

Every chapter will guide you to balance the commercial side of making profits every day, directly or indirectly. Thus, the book covers important topics like Client and Staff Retention, Vendor Relationship Management to Smart Marketing and Franchising. It also covers how easily you can Handle an Unsatisfied Client and make use of Mystery Shopping for Auditing. And I have added the important chapters on both Artificial Intelligence for The New You and Analysing Your Growth in each step.

I promise that once you read, understand and follow this approach, you will not only witness a positive environment but also enjoy profitable results every day.

Happy reading! And for sure ...Happy Sales!!

# ABOUT THE AUTHOR

Gunjann Taneja is amongst India's top trainers in product & skill knowledge in the beauty industry. She has conducted numerous workshops and training programs for popular brands such as Dabur, The Body Shop, Amway, etc. She believes in learning a new skill every year and thus holds more than **25 certificates** in various skills related to beauty and hair treatment.

She has served as a guest faculty at several institutes for over two decades, imparting knowledge on various topics related to the beauty industry. She visits as a **Guest Lecturer at Delhi University for Salon Management and Retail Marketing.** She is also actively involved in **designing the Curriculum Framework for various Vocational Courses** in beauty & salon management in Polytechnics.

As a Permanent Makeup Expert, she has **worked with Bollywood Celebrities, Super Models, Prominent Beauty Brands** and virtually the who's who of society. With over 26 years of experience in amalgamating salon & education, Gunjann is also a **Celebrity Trainer, Columnist as well as a Permanent Makeup Expert with many Cancer Foundation NGOs.**

Gunjann is also a "Serial Salon Opener" and holds a record for opening 50 Franchisee centres in a short span of one year for her **own brand "Bharti Taneja's Alps Salon & Academy".** She is also well versed in Developing Skin & Hair Care Products with many years of experience in the laboratory as well as her **production factory in Delhi,** where she manufactures these products for various third-party companies as well. Besides making excellent food at home she also **formulates** a wide range of more than **150 kinds of Skin and Hair Care Products** as a part of her menu.

Gunjann is a **popular columnist** for several magazines, dailies & online portals. Her popular beauty **shows on Television & Radio** have won her a legion of fans. Her contribution to the beauty industry as an educationist has been phenomenal. She has **represented India in the Commonwealth Asia Makeup Competition** as well as make up jury for many events including those of **B&WSSC**. She has been a **Guest**

**Speaker in Salon Management Congress** each year and spoken on various topics concerning **Salon Management and Franchising in the Beauty Industry.**

Armed with a **Diploma in Rhetoric Writing from Harvard University** she finally fulfilled her dream of writing a series of books on salon management. With her books, she hopes to spread an understanding that beauty salons are not just an industry of facial treatments, hair cut or make up…it goes deeper and encompasses much more than that!

As **Vice President of the Chamber of Trade Industry, Vice President of Women Empowerment in the Global Chamber of Consumer Rights,** and **Lecturer at the University of Delhi,** Gunjann's reach extends far beyond salons.

She has also served for almost a year as the **India Business and Technical Head at Naturals Beauty Academy** and has authored almost all the **books of Naturals Beauty Academy.** Her skill at **designing the Curriculum for Naturals** and introducing the academies with new technologies every month made such a lasting impression, that when she visited **College of Coimbatore,** they offered her a position as **Board Member for Education.** Gunjann has also designed few self-beauty courses on the **online platform of IIT MADRAS.** She has spent a year as the **COO of Naturals Skill Development and Training Centre (NSTC) India** where she planned and executed many projects including with the **Governments of Tamil Nadu and Karnataka** as also **designed many SOPs for more than 800 plus Salons**.

Last but not the least, she also holds a **World Record** for makeup by performing **345 makeups in just a span of 2 hours,** with her small team.

Her mantra,

**"Money in my pocket, Knowledge in my mind, Kindness in my heart, Confidence on my face and Responsibilities in my soul, all these make me who I am!",**

keeps her grounded despite all her achievements!

# INDEX

**Chapter 1:** Keep Them Coming Back: **Client Retention:** ................................15

Celebrate Their Special Days and Shower Them with Offers
Why Are Birthday Offers So Important?
Regular Monthly Offers – How Do They Work?
Listen More and Talk Less
How to get your team on board
Give More Than Promised
The Latest in Services and Products
Few Simple Tips to Stay Updated

**Chapter 2:** Happy Team, Happy Salon: **Retaining Your Staff:** ......................29

Give Salaries on Time
Give Incentives with Achievable Goals
Introduce Trainings Every Quarter
Why Should We Train Staff Regularly?
The Other Side of the Coin: The Risk of Staff Leaving
Give and Get Respect
Don't Make Them Feel Irreplaceable or Indispensable

**Chapter 3:** Turning Products into Profits: **Retail Magic:** .................................45

Sell the Right Product
Client Education & Empowerment
Effective Communication
Sell but do not oversell
Positive approach
Let's Categorise The Products
Important Points To Consider While Selling Retail Products
How Every Product Sold, Adds To The Economy Of The System
The Bigger Picture

**Chapter 4:** Building Strong Partnerships: **Vendor Management:** .............57

Structured Vendor Relationship
Vendor Selection Criteria
Contractual Agreements
Performance Metrics
Assessing Demand and Inventory Needs
Setting Budget and Financial Considerations
Identifying Preferred Vendors

Establishing Order Frequency and Lead Times
Reviewing and Updating the Plan
Evaluating Vendors

**Chapter 5:** Oops Moments: **Dealing with an Upset Client:** ........................65

Don't be scared
Take the client to a quiet room
Serve her water
Listen Attentively and Stay Calm
Apologize Sincerely
Find a Solution or Offer Compensation
Follow-Up After the Visit
How to Balance the Staff who has made the mistake

**Chapter 6:** Who's Watching? **The Power of Mystery Shopping:** ................73

Choosing the Right Auditor
Know the End Result You Want from the Audit
Important Considerations
Areas to Focus on During the Audit
Specific Points to Investigate
The Final Question
Repeat Regularly
Decide on the Frequency
Key Guidelines for Regular Audits
Discuss the Audit and Take Action
Positive Audit Results
Negative Audit Results
Key Actionable Steps

**Chapter 7:** A Salon Revolution: **Artificial Intelligence & You:**......................91

Data and Records at Your Fingertips
Why it matters
Smart Feedback Filtering: How AI Saves Your Salon's Reputation
How It Works
This Gives You a Second Chance
Booking Appointments Through Your Website
Salary Calculation Made Easy with AI

**Chapter 8:** Marketing Moves That Matter: **Smart Marketing:** ...................101

Know your Target Audience
Analyse the market every month
Marketing Tips & Tricks for a Salon

**Chapter 9:** Thinking Bigger? **Let's Talk Franchising:** ....................................111

Types of Franchising Models in the Salon Industry
Why a Salon Should Franchise
Make the Franchise Plan Viable and Competitive
Draft the Legal Papers Well and Abide by Them
Regular Observation of Franchise Reports
Remember they are your partners and not your employees

**Chapter 10:** Are You Growing? **Let's Measure It:** ............................................125

Use Audit to Catch Leakages Monthly
Invest in a financial advisor
Pay regular taxes
Give yourself a salary
Take corrective action without delaying

**And this is the new beginning: Letter from the Author**

# CHAPTER 1

# KEEP THEM COMING BACK: CLIENT RETENTION

## Celebrate Their Special Days and Shower Them with Offers

Who doesn't love to be wished on their special day? And when that wish comes with a bonus, such as a discount on the beauty services they regularly enjoy at your salon, it feels like the perfect gift. Whether your client is celebrating her birthday with a quiet family dinner or throwing a big party with friends and loved ones, she will likely need salon services in the days leading up to the event.

To make her day even better, be sure to call 15 days in advance to remind her to book her beauty and hair services, and offer her options for a hair blow dry or makeup on her birthday. Calling her in advance may also make her try few extra services. A simple message on the special day itself will put a smile on her face. Plan ahead for business, and use her special day to bond by sending her a birthday wish.

## Why Are Birthday Offers So Important?

### 1. Emotional Bonding:

Wishing a client on her birthday creates a special emotional connection. It makes her feel valued, and it shows that you care about her beyond just business. This personal touch strengthens the bond between you and the client. So, don't just call her and wish her. Keep a friendly conversation. Glance her past visit record and discuss about that. make sure that the call is from heart and I am sure, she will feel the connect and visit. When I was a manager, I use to even note, smallest things like, this client loves rose flowers, and convey on the phone, "when you will come this time for the makeup, I have kept aside a lovely rose accessory, I am sure you will love that in your hair. It is like a small gift from our side." I know she will come, pay for hair style and make up, and would smile every time even in future, when she sees that accessory in her cupboard. That's an example of building the bond.

### 2. Increased Loyalty:

A birthday wish can enhance client loyalty. In a world where people often receive messages through WhatsApp and other social media platforms, a phone call to personally wish her can make a huge difference. Many clients will appreciate the gesture and feel more connected to your salon. Now days, you have the facility of designing a personal card through app, which makes her feel special. And she will be regular with you.

### 3. Increased Business Potential:

By calling 15 days before her birthday, you create an opportunity for her to visit before the day arrives to take advantage of the birthday discount. During this visit, she might opt for an upgraded service because of the discount, making it the perfect opportunity for an upsell. Whether it's a new haircut, a facial to tackle fine lines, or other services she's been thinking about, this emotional month is the right time to suggest something new. This not only boosts her confidence but also generates extra revenue for your business. "I know Mrs Sharma, you always go for a regular facial, this time on your birthday, try our gold one. It will make a huge difference in the results." I am sure, if the bond is there, she will spend some extra rupees.

### 4. Positive Online Reviews:

Clients are more likely to leave positive reviews on social media when they've been surprised with a special offer. Since it's her special day, the emotional impact of this gesture can encourage her to share her experience, bringing in new clients and increasing your salon's visibility. Make sure you make her video, and ask her permission to post that. An emotional testimonial is much more effective than an influencer's recommendation.

## Regular Monthly Offers – How Do They Work?

Besides birthday wishes, regular offers can indirectly boost salon sales in several effective ways. Here's why:

### 1. Increased Loyalty:

Clients who know that new offers are available each month are more likely to return regularly. They will appreciate the salon's constant updates with new products and services, and they'll be excited to try out special discounts. They'll also look forward to receiving surprise discounts on their regular services, particularly during festive months. After all, what woman doesn't love sales and discounts?

### 2. Encouraging Upsells for Less Popular Services:

Monthly offers can be designed to encourage clients to try services they might not usually consider, such as body polish or nail art. By offering discounts on these services, you can introduce clients to new treatments, and they might incorporate them into their regular visits. As these services enhance their overall look, they're more likely to get noticed and complimented by friends, leading to word-of-mouth recommendations.

### 3. Boosting Revenue on Low-Volume Days:

There are certain days, such as mid-week or during slow seasons like the monsoon or summer heat, that tend to have lower sales. During these times, a special "Monsoon Sale" or "Summer Cooler Offer" can help boost business and prevent losses. For homemakers who might prefer quieter times, offering additional discounts or happy hour deals (such as from 12:00 noon to 4:00 pm) can attract clients and increase revenue during off-peak hours.

### Points to Remember:

**• Offer Different Services or Products Each Month:**

Keep your offers fresh by introducing new services or products every month. They should not be so predictable that the client finds the pattern and waits for the offer instead of coming and spending regularly. This is one of the most important point to remember. If the client gets the pattern, the sales will be reduced to particular months only. So, design carefully.

- **Make It Simple and Easy to Redeem:**

Ensure that your clients can easily redeem the offers, making the process smooth and hassle-free. I have personally seen, many at times the offer will say," buy this, earn these many points, each point is equal to this much amount, and after particular amount these services would be free". Not only for me, but the rest of the world too, this might sound like a tongue twister. The client gets encouraged when she sees an offer that she can understand and feel that she has save this much amount by spending a little more or by choosing the right service for herself. So, make sound easy and calculative for the client, as well as the workers who are recommending it to the client. "Buy this, get this Free. Flat 30 % off for today on these services". You will see more conversions in these than the complicated ones.

- **Promote Through Multiple Channels:**

It's an era which needs to be influenced 360 degree. With everything reachable on the mobile, I sometimes feel that the sale in some cases belongs to fastest fingers first. Use text messages, emails, and Instagram stories to market your offers to clients, ensuring they are aware and excited to take advantage of the offer. Thus plan your budget in a way, that you spend more, in lesser time, and in different categories, to cover it all.

- **Track Offer Performance:**

Keep a record of which offers perform better than others. How many clients got attracted in ratio to how many finally got converted and opted for the same. This will allow you to plan more effectively and run even better offers in the future. I remember once, instead of giving flat 25% off on bridal make up, we kept a Cinderella shoe on display, and said, if it fits you, you get 25% off on bridal make up. People in the exhibition queued up for the same, and once they got the discount, they booked the make up with us. They knew that we were good in our make-up skill, but this offer was attractive and each one of them got a feeling of pride in winning or rather the getting it. So, schemes like this help increasing sales with added fun!

## Listen More and Talk Less

In my experience visiting various salons and conducting Mystery Audits as a client, the ones that truly caught my attention were those where the staff had the patience to listen attentively. They first understood my requirement and then guided me to the best solution. Anything less than this level of attentiveness would not have appealed to me. The same is true for any client.

Today's clients are well-informed - they've already researched the solutions to their problems online before booking an appointment. They don't need you to lecture them; they want to talk to you and hear a solution that aligns with their own ideas. They feel that they already know the answer and are judging whether you aware about it. And in addition calculating once you start talking whether are you skilled enough to execute the same? The key to making effective recommendations lies in paying 100% attention to what the client says and 200% attention to the subtle hints within their words. What do they like? What do they dislike? What really matters to them? Understanding these details is crucial, and it can only be done when the manager, or any staff member, listens intently, without interrupting. Thereafter analyses, recommends and also knows that the team can execute the treatment as desired and promised.

**The golden rule of sales is simple:**

*"Listen to her for 10 minutes, and she will follow you for the next 10."*

She will know that you're offering the right guidance, and in return, she will trust your advice. If you reverse this approach and talk too much without listening first, you might hear, "Oh, actually, I was expecting something else," and that, is a conversation you want to avoid.

## Here's how you can get your team on board with this approach:

### 1. Hold a Small Staff Meeting

Emphasize the importance of listening to improve the client experience. Help your staff understand that better listening equals fewer mistakes, less stress, and ultimately, better reviews. Make sure, to do these meeting as often as weekly or bi monthly. Listening is a habit, which is not practiced by many, so this needs to be introduced, time to time.

### 2. Use Real Examples & Roleplays

Conduct mock consultations (MOCs) to show the team how the experience changes when they listen more and speak only when necessary. Incorporating fun, short roleplays in staff meetings can help them feel the difference, rather than just hearing about it. Small drills like these, make them remember forever, rather than just listening and agreeing half-heartedly. Remember as a child we use to say:

*"I hear, I forget*
*I see and I remember*
*I do and I understand"*

### 3. Highlight the Importance of Consultation

While skill is crucial, a solid consultation process is just as important in helping clients choose the salon, technician, and service. If your team can master the art of consultation, they'll be able to offer more personalized, accurate recommendations. Consultation also plays a big role in handling the situation the after the process, in case results are not achieved as expected. When I did the hair colour course by L'Oréal, I understood how to overshadow one colour over the other, but simultaneously saw if too much pre lightening is done, it effects the hair health. Thus, by conducting a strand test, we could see if the hair would get sensitised and brittle. So even if the client would want blond streaks on hair with henna, it was the power of both the knowledge and consultation, which enabled me and my team to convince her for another shade that would suit her, while maintaining her hair conditions post the head wash. On the other hand, if the team lacked the power of consultation, it would have resulted in the client with either the wrong shade on her head of a head full of dry brittle hair. So, it is important to spread the knowledge as consultation to the client, rather than to stay mum and spoil the result.

**4. Introduce Helpful Techniques**

- **L.A.S.T. Technique:**

    o **Listen** – Let the client speak fully before responding.

    o **Acknowledge** – Use affirming words like "Hmm," "Yes, I understand," or "I get it."

    o **Summarize** – Repeat back their key points to ensure you understand, e.g., "So, you're looking for a subtle red highlight that's not too bold?"

    o **Talk** – Once you've fully listened and analysed, offer your professional input.

- **80/20 Rule:** Encourage your staff to listen 80% of the time and talk only 20%. This approach fosters trust, builds rapport, and ensures that you have all the information needed before offering suggestions.

By adopting these techniques and encouraging more listening than talking, you will create an environment where clients feel heard and respected. In turn, this will lead to greater satisfaction, increased loyalty, and better reviews for your salon.

## Give More Than Promised

When a client visits your salon, she comes with certain expectations. After discussing her needs with the manager and technician, she expects at least an 80% result to be satisfied. Now, imagine if you deliver more than 120%. This will undoubtedly delight her, and she'll be eager to praise your salon to everyone she knows.

The key here is to always promise realistic, professional outcomes that you can consistently deliver. Overpromising can backfire, but delivering more than expected can make all the difference.

### 1. The WOW Factor

Picture this: You promise a good service and deliver something even better. This surprise "Wow!" moment creates a lasting impression. It's the kind of experience that turns a one-time visit into a loyal relationship. For example, if a client is waiting for her facial and you send a pedicurist, who was anyways sitting idle to offer a complimentary quick shoulder massage, she will not only feel relaxed but will leave glowing. These extra touches create a memorable experience. I remember, my father going to the same barber, because he use to give a couple of minutes face massage, complimentary with haircut. It is as simple as this, and he was regular with them for a decade.

### 2. Building Indirect Trust

Always keep in mind that every bit counts. When you deliver more than promised, clients naturally perceive it as a sign of confidence and professionalism. Going beyond expectations through detailed consultations and thoughtful service reinforces their trust and leaves a lasting impression, building the foundation of strong client relationships.

Clients will recognize and appreciate the extra effort you put into their experience. They'll realize that you genuinely care about how they feel, not just how they look. By consistently going above and beyond, you build trust - something far more powerful than any marketing strategy.

### 3. Word of Mouth

People love to share a good surprise. When you exceed a client's expectations, she's more likely to tell her friends and family. These small moments of over-delivery can turn into valuable referrals and positive social media reviews. And as we all know, if a client is recommended to a particular salon by her best friend or a close relative, the trust factor builds in automatically. That personal endorsement carries significant weight, often making the client more open to recommendations and confident in the salon's expertise. This inherent trust, combined with a strong consultation process, sets the stage for long-term loyalty and satisfaction.

## Value Add: The Latest in Services and Products

The fashion and beauty industries evolve rapidly. Every few months, new facials, manicure kits, and techniques emerge in the market. Staying updated in the beauty and hair industry isn't just a good idea—it's essential for staying competitive, innovative, and trusted by your clients. Imagine a client asks about a new service, and you have no idea what they're talking about. That moment could cause the client to slip away quietly, choosing a salon that's more knowledgeable and can answer all their questions with confidence.

Here's why keeping up with new product launches, tools, and techniques will level up your salon:

### 1. Clients Google Everything

Today's clients are incredibly well-informed—they're scrolling through Instagram, TikTok, and YouTube, following influencers and keeping up with the latest trends. They'll expect you to know about these new techniques and products. If you're not updated, the trust factor with your client will diminish. They'll think, "If they're not aware of this new trend, how can they customize it for me?" This might drive them to another salon that's flaunting the latest techniques online.

### 2. Study Ahead and Become a Pioneer

Being the first to introduce a trending product or service in your local area sets your salon apart as modern, stylish, and knowledgeable. Clients will associate your brand with expertise and leadership in the beauty space. When they see positive results from others, they'll trust you to deliver the same. Staying ahead of trends makes you the go-to salon for cutting-edge beauty services.

### 3. Revenue Boost

Launching new products and services gives clients a fresh reason to book appointments and purchase retail items. When they try the latest trend at your salon, they're likely to share it on social media, creating a buzz. This generates free publicity, brings in new clients, and increases daily revenue. A viral video of a client showing off their new look can attract attention and drive even more business to your salon. Few days back, when Korean hair spa was the talk of town, I saw influencers posting that they got the appointment for the service after waiting for a week. This proves, how the new viral service was not only creating a buzz, but was also adding business to the salon throughout the month.

### 4. Staff Motivation

Offering new services and techniques keeps your staff engaged and motivated. Regularly upgrading their knowledge and skills is crucial for staff retention. Training your team on the latest trends makes work more enjoyable, inspires creativity, and boosts confidence during client consultations. It also helps them stay excited about learning and evolving with the industry. They love to flaunt this knowledge in front of client and also their friends working in another salon. This indirectly helps in staff retention and easy recruitment of the new ones when needed.

## Here Are Few Simple Tips to Stay Updated:

- **WFollow Industry Leaders:** Stay inspired by following top beauty professionals, educators, and influencers on social media. Learn from them, innovate, and repeat the process. Remember, that they can show what is the latest in the market, but don't think you know fully. While getting influenced, buy the product, undergo the training and then execute the same on the client. Every bit involves in touch in touching the skin or the hair of the clint, do it only when you are certified and confident.

- **Attend Beauty Trade Shows & Webinars:** Participate in trade shows and webinars throughout the year to see what's new and upcoming in the industry. They are the best way to become aware of upcoming launches. The live demos happening on the stage throughout the day also make you confident of the results. This is not only to educate you, but to inspire you and many others about the advancement in the industry.

- **Read Beauty Magazines & Blogs:** Dedicate time to reading online beauty magazines and blogs. Staying informed will help you answer your clients' questions and stay on top of industry trends. Spare a few hours every week, dedicated to read about what the industry experts are saying and then implement the techniques you read or hear about. Magazines, blogs, TEDX talks, or a YouTube channel of beauty, make sure you follow and learn both the new launches and the myths of the markets.

- **Collaborate with Brands:** Work with product brands and invite their representatives to demonstrate new launches. If they know you're interested, many will offer free demos and training sessions. This is the best way to train yourself and your team with no extra cost. With the rising competition in the market, almost every brand is doing the same.

**The Bottom Line:**

Never stop learning. This mindset has been my personal motto for 26 years. Over the years, I've completed 30 courses, attended over 100 seminars, and read countless beauty magazines. When I read, I stay unbiased and just absorb everything the company and the expert is saying, even if I am not a big fan of the individual. Staying updated with the latest trends in products and services is what keeps me going, and it has truly shaped my career. It's a continuous process that pays off, and I plan to keep doing it for as long as I can.

# CHAPTER 2

# HAPPY TEAM, HAPPY SALON: RETAINING YOUR STAFF

## Give Salaries on Time

It's often said that money drives the world. The foundation of the relationship between you and your staff lies in timely salary payments. Ensuring that salaries are paid on time is essential for maintaining a positive and productive environment in your salon. If you wait until the end of the month to start worrying about salaries, it's too late. Plan for it at the beginning of the month to ensure there's no stress when payday arrives. Here's why timely salary payments are crucial:

### 1. Salary on Time is the Foundation of Trust

Paying salaries on time is a key factor in winning your staff's trust. When staff members know they can rely on you to pay them promptly, it builds a sense of security and respect. I remember my parents saying, "My kids can buy anything on the 11th, the day after payday. Before that, even a safety pin feels expensive." At the time, I didn't understand, but once I started earning, I realized how vital timely payments are. Paying on time shows your team that you value their work and respect their time, which in turn encourages loyalty and boosts their performance.

### 2. Delaying Pay Causes Unnecessary Stress

If you have a set salary date, it's essential to plan your finances around it. Delayed payments cause stress among staff members, which can distract them from their work and diminish their ability to provide excellent customer service. In a service-based industry like a salon, a happy and focused staff directly translates to happy clients. Indeed, you may also feel like not facing the staff or avoiding them in a few cases, as you are scared that they might ask about the salary directly, and you don't want to be in the unavoidable situation where you have to make an excuse for it.

**Always remember this easy calculation in any industry:**

*Happy Staff = Happy Clients.*

### 3. It Contributes to High Staff Morale

A team that receives their salary on time feels respected and valued. This boosts morale and motivates them to go the extra mile for your clients. Timely payments are a sign that you appreciate the time and effort they put into their work, and that recognition goes a long way in maintaining high staff engagement and productivity. In our Salon, we had the rule of paying the basic salary to the staff on 10th and the incentives every Monday. How excited were they, to receive that money and plan their weekly off, sometimes involving that extra cash.

### 4. Helps in Staff Retention

If your staff becomes accustomed to delayed payments, they will likely seek employment elsewhere. While occasional delays are understandable, a consistent pattern of late payments will lead to dissatisfaction and a high turnover rate. Word spreads quickly, and former employees may mention late payments as the reason for their departure, thus spreading it in the market. They may say the same thing to the new joining making it harder to retain talent. It's better to prioritize timely salary payments to keep your trained and experienced staff happy and loyal.

### 5. Avoid Legal Issues

Failing to pay on time can lead to legal consequences. If staff members are consistently paid late, they may take legal action. Labor laws are strict, even in countries like India, and not adhering to these regulations could lead to legal complications, reputational damage, and unnecessary financial burden. Avoid such situations by planning your finances properly and ensuring that salaries are paid on time.

**Another Formula Says:**

*Timely Salary Payments = Happier Staff = Successful Business*

This version improves the flow of information and highlights the importance of timely payments for a productive and harmonious work environment.

## Give Incentives with Achievable Goals

In the beauty industry, performance is often driven by targets and incentives. Setting achievable goals for your staff creates motivation, pushing them to reach those targets. Once they achieve these goals and are rewarded, they become a self-driven sales force. However, it's important that these goals and incentives are clear, attainable, and aligned with both individual and salon objectives.

**Here's how achievable incentives can positively impact your salon's sales and overall atmosphere:**

### 1. Motivation Comes Naturally

Rewarding your staff for their performance is one of the strongest motivators to boost their sales efforts. When incentives are challenging yet attainable, they encourage your staff to go the extra mile - whether it's recommending products, upselling services, or making clients aware of your salon's full range of offerings. My formula for motivating them was to tell them every day , how much extra money they have made on that day before they leave. That made a difference, as when they performed well, they were happy and if they felt they didn't perform that day, they got self-motivated for the next day.

### 2. Fosters Healthy Competition

Incentives can foster a healthy competitive environment, but it's essential to maintain a balance. Competition should be about elevating everyone's performance, not about putting others down. As a manager, you need to remain unbiased and encourage teamwork. Daily motivational sessions can help keep the energy high and ensure that competition remains positive. Celebrate achievements in morning meetings. You will be surprised how just a simple act of "the team clapping for the highest achiever" can motivate others for next day. Remember, acknowledge improvements on a daily basis - not just at the end of the month.

### 3. Staff Takes Interest in Learning

When staff knows they have targets to meet, they are more likely to invest time in learning about the products and services they're selling. They will understand the unique selling points (USPs) of each product, which, in turn, will make them more confident about recommending the right services and products to clients. As a result, they may start combining services (e.g., a manicure with a pedicure or a facial with face bleach) to improve both their sales and the client experience. You will see the whole game changing from you pushing the staff to train more, to them getting eager to learn something more.

### 4. Focus on Selling the Right Products

It's important that the incentives are aligned with genuine recommendations based on the client's needs, rather than simply pushing products to meet a target. For instance, you wouldn't try to sell a comb to a bald person. Instead, recommend a hair growth treatment and perhaps gift the comb once they see results. Selling should be about building trust with the client and recommending products and services that truly benefit them. It is very important to make sure that they are on the right track of recommendation and not just on a lookout to achieve the sales target. If you don't keep a check on each recommendation, you might lose a client once she feels over pressurised or given a wrong service/product to achieve the targets. It is important to remember that the clients could also be working in a similar environment of sales and targets in a different industry and might be easily able to differentiate between the right recommendations and the act of only pushing sales. Once a client feels cheated on this score, she will never return for another service.

### 5. Retention of Top Performers

Staff who consistently achieve their targets and are rewarded for their efforts are less likely to leave. Many salons incentivize staff weekly, paying out cash that they can spend on their days off. This not only motivates them but also reduces staff turnover. By offering regular incentives, you foster a sense of satisfaction that encourages employees to stay longer.

### 6. Sales Increase Dramatically

Clear and measurable goals for incentives create consistency in sales. When staff knows exactly what they need to do to earn a reward, they are more likely to stay focused and motivated. This repeatable process can lead to long-term improvements in sales, and in many cases, you'll see a significant increase in retail sales.

### 7. Products Encourage Clients to Revisit

Selling products that become part of a client's daily routine helps remind them to return to your salon. They know once the overnight cream finishes, it is the time for my next facial. It is important that you not only teach them about the products, but also about regular use of the products. For example, a face wash kept on the bathroom sink is more likely to be used regularly than one stored in a cupboard. Likewise, anti-wrinkle creams kept on the bedside table are used more often than those stored out of sight. This simple input given to a client, about correct positioning of products in visible and accessible places, encourages reordering and repeat visits to the salon.

### 8. Change Targets Regularly

Varying your targets keeps things fresh and challenges staff to expand their skill set. Targets can include selling a particular product, recommending a new service, booking packages, or getting clients to leave 5-star reviews on Google. Regularly changing targets ensures that staff members continue to grow and develop new skills, keeping them engaged and motivated.

### 9. Get Creative with Rewards

Incentives don't always have to be monetary. Occasionally, you can reward the team with something that promotes teamwork, such as a group outing or a movie night. For more competitive incentives, monetary rewards are effective. Offering unique rewards like a paid holiday trip for top performers - where staff can take a spouse or partner - adds a personal touch that can motivate employees to work even harder. Imagine the pride a beautician will have, if you give her a holiday trip with spouse. The whole house will make her feel special, and they will also value you and the work environment.

### 10. Clear and Creative Communication

Staff will feel demotivated if goals and rewards are unclear. It's essential that you communicate exactly what the targets are and how they can be achieved. If there's any confusion about the goals, it can lead to frustration, and the staff may lose motivation. Ensure that targets are well explained, so everyone understands what's expected and how they'll be rewarded.

By setting clear, measurable, and realistic goals for your staff, you'll cultivate a culture of healthy competition, motivation, and teamwork. This will lead to improved sales, better overall performance, and a more positive salon environment.

## Introduce Trainings Every Quarter

In an industry that evolves rapidly with new technologies, products, and techniques, regular staff training is essential. Consistently investing in your salon team not only keeps them updated on the latest trends but also helps improve service quality, builds confidence, and ensures that your business stays competitive.

However, there's always the risk that trained employees may seek better opportunities elsewhere. Balancing these two aspects - staff development and minimizing attrition - requires careful planning.

Training your salon staff is essential to maintaining high-quality services, boost client satisfaction, and stay competitive. While there is always the risk that trained employees may leave, this can be mitigated by fostering a positive work culture, offering competitive salaries, creating growth opportunities, and introducing retention incentives. By finding the right balance, you can continue investing in your staff's development while ensuring that they feel motivated to stay with your salon long-term.

First let's explore the importance of regular training and how to handle the associated risks effectively.

## Why Should We Train Staff Regularly?

### 1. Keep Them Updated

The beauty industry is constantly evolving with new tools, techniques, and products. Regular training ensures that your staff is equipped with the latest skills and knowledge. For example, imagine if a client has dry skin and the staff doesn't know about the latest products containing AHA and BHA. They may end up using a standard moisturizer that won't address the client's specific needs. Regular training prevents this and ensures your staff is always informed and capable.

### 2. Better Service Means Happier Clients

Clients often see salon staff as the experts in skincare and hair care. They expect knowledgeable professionals who can deliver results. Regular training helps your staff stay on top of trends and improve their skills, enabling them to provide the high-quality service that clients expect. Well-trained staff can also offer expert advice, which enhances the overall client experience and satisfaction.

### 3. Boosts Staff Confidence

Confidence plays a crucial role in delivering exceptional service. A confident stylist or therapist can answer clients' questions with ease and provide the best recommendations. As clients become more informed, they expect staff to be equally knowledgeable. If the staff isn't adequately trained, they may struggle to address questions or concerns, leading to dissatisfaction. Regular training helps your team stay confident and capable, ensuring they meet client expectations and build trust.

### 4. Continuous Learning Promotes Professional Growth

Continuous learning keeps employees engaged, motivated, and growing professionally. With regular training, they can learn new skills, refine existing ones, and become more competent in their roles. This not only leads to improved performance but also contributes to higher job satisfaction and retention rates.

### 5. Enhances Salon Reputation

Well-trained staff enhances your salon's reputation. Clients notice when a salon's team is professional, knowledgeable, and up-to-date with trends. Training also catches the attention of retail brands, who may want to include your salon in their annual training programs. As a result, your salon will shine in the industry, further boosting your brand's reputation.

## The Other Side of the Coin: The Risk of Staff Leaving

While regular training is crucial, there's always the possibility that trained employees may leave for better opportunities. I often hear salon owners complaining about this - about how they invested on education of the team and the team members left in a few months. Here are some ways to minimize this risk while ensuring your salon benefits from ongoing staff development:

### 1. Create a Positive Work Environment

Employees are more likely to stay with a company that values them and fosters a positive atmosphere. When you invest in their training and development, make sure the environment remains supportive and encouraging. Recognition, appreciation, and healthy competition will help increase job satisfaction, making employees feel valued and less likely to leave.

### 2. Offer Competitive Salaries

As staff skills improve, it's essential to adjust their salaries to match their growing expertise. Don't base their salary on what they were paid when they first joined the salon. Instead, ensure that their pay reflects their upgraded skills and market value. If your staff feel underpaid compared to the industry standard, they may seek better opportunities elsewhere. Offering competitive salaries helps retain skilled employees and prevents turnover. I have seen, a beautician joining a slon, getting paid as a beautician 's salary even after a year, while now she is also performing make up and skin treatments which she has learnt. Post one year, she meets a friend of Her's with the same skill earning much more than her , and she easily gets poached away. Alon owners are ready to give more salary to a new employee, but are not ready to increase the salary of the old employee, as per the market norms. Then you are bound to lose them any day and will be left feeling betrayed of training them latest and they leaving you for few rupees, which even you could have offered.

### 3. Introduce a Loyalty Program

Loyalty programs for staff can incentivize them to stay with your salon. A reward system for reaching milestones, such as completing a year with the company, can go a long way in retaining employees. These rewards should be motivational and achievable, providing an additional reason for staff to remain with the company. Add slabs in the loyalty programme like if you complete one year you get this, in three this and above five this. With such an incentive program in place, when your staff knows that the annual milestone award can be won after a few months, it encourages them to stay on for a few months more and so on. And in no time will you see them in your company for decades together.

### 4. Offer Regular Promotions

Career growth opportunities within the salon can also help retain trained staff. If staff see that there is potential for advancement - from junior stylist to senior stylist, trainer, or even head of department - they will be more likely to stay and continue their development within the same company. Regular promotions provide clear growth paths and motivate employees to keep improving their skills. They should be aware about the same and must aspire to reach the next level associated with the growth in skillset.

### 5. Make Them Feel Like Family

When employees feel like they are part of a supportive, family-like environment, they are less likely to leave. Respect their knowledge, involve them in decision-making, and celebrate milestones like birthdays. Small gestures like acknowledging personal achievements and offering condolences in times of loss can go a long way in making staff feel connected to the salon. When they feel truly valued, they are less likely to be tempted by outside opportunities. This I learned from my mom who used to wish every employee on their Birthdays, and ensured she talks to them for 5 mins on that day. And the result is there for us to see – today we have staff who have been with us for 2 and even 3 decades.

## Give and Get Respect

As the owner or leader of the salon, it's understood that you are at the top of the hierarchy. However, showing respect to your staff goes beyond simply acknowledging your position. A respectful environment fosters trust, loyalty, and a stronger team dynamic.

Respect is a two-way street in any workplace. By listening actively, offering growth opportunities, empowering your staff, being transparent, and showing appreciation, you create a positive environment where your team feels valued and motivated. Conducting thoughtful exit interviews if needed, ensures that even when staff members leave, you learn from the experience and maintain a positive culture. Ultimately, fostering mutual respect will create a stronger, more loyal team and a thriving salon.

**Let me explain each point by explaining how to show respect to your staff in day-to-day interactions:**

### 1. Listen Actively

Holding regular group meetings and bi-monthly one-on-one sessions with your team is essential. During these meetings, make sure to actively listen to what your staff has to say. This could include their concerns, suggestions, or feedback. Give them the space to speak, and take note of important points. During these conversations, keep a neutral expression and avoid making any immediate decisions or reactions. This ensures that your staff knows their opinions are valued and that their concerns are being taken seriously. And yes, like we do with the client, as I've brought out earlier, listen more, give no expression and talk less.

### 2. Offer Growth Opportunities

Your staff will remain loyal if they see clear career advancement paths within the salon. By offering opportunities for professional growth—such as promotion to senior stylist, trainer, or manager - you help your employees see that they have a future with your business. Providing skill development opportunities demonstrates that you care about their long-term success and value their contributions.

### 3. Empower Your Staff

For many individuals in the beauty industry, working as a stylist or beautician is not just a job - it's an opportunity for empowerment. Many women choose this career despite societal pressures, often feeling undervalued in comparison to others in more conventional roles. As a leader, it's crucial to motivate and empower your staff by helping them see the value of their work. I always remind them that just as doctors heal the body, they heal the skin, hair, and confidence of their clients. For the clients who visit them to solve their skin or hair problems, they are the doctors. When staff feel respected and confident in their abilities, their performance improves, and they become more invested in their work and clients. Empower your team and encourage them to see themselves as professionals who are equal to other respected careers. This is the same feeling they take with them into their homes and amongst their friends, and indeed the whole world will start valuing beauty as a noble career.

### 4. Be Transparent and Fair

Transparency and fairness are key to earning the respect of your staff. Ensure that everyone is treated equally, whether it's in terms of pay structure, commission plans, or career advancement opportunities. If employees perceive favouritism or inconsistency in how they are treated, it can lead to frustration and a lack of trust. And once this sets in, it is difficult to remove from the system and their thoughts. So be extra careful not to indulge in the same. By being open and fair about all aspects of the job, you will encourage loyalty and respect among your staff.

### 5. Appreciate Their Efforts

Regularly acknowledge the efforts of your staff, no matter how small. A simple "thank you" or a gesture like ringing a gratitude bell for every good deed can create a positive atmosphere in your salon. Showing appreciation not only boosts morale but also motivates your team to continue working hard and supporting each other. When staff feel recognized and valued, it fosters a positive work culture and inspires them to strive for excellence.

### 6. Conduct Exit Interviews & ensure Employees Leave on Good Terms

When a staff member decides to leave, it's important to conduct an exit interview. This gives you insights into the reasons for their departure and helps you identify areas for improvement. It also allows you to maintain a positive relationship with departing employees, and if they leave on good terms, they may be open to returning in the future. Creating a positive exit process can encourage others to follow suit, resigning respectfully and with proper notice. On the other hand, making the departure process difficult or sarcastic can encourage a culture of resignation without notice, which can hurt your business in the long run. They would feel that without notice quitting is easier than everyday sarcasm and thus no one would let you know when they plan to leave, landing you in the difficult situation any day.

## Don't Make Them Feel Irreplaceable or Indispensable

While it's important for your salon staff to feel valued and empowered, it's equally important that they don't feel irreplaceable. When employees start believing they are irreplaceable, it can disrupt the balance of the team dynamics and even foster a sense of entitlement. However, as a leader, you may fear upsetting the balance when you have to address difficult situations.

**Let's explore how you can maintain morale while ensuring no one feels above the team:**

### 1. Appreciate the Team, Not Just the Individual

Shift the focus towards celebrating the team as a whole rather than singling out individuals repeatedly. Even if one employee stands out for their excellence, it's important to emphasize teamwork and collaboration. By doing so, you avoid creating a culture where one person feels more important than others. However, it's important to introduce this shift early on, rather than after a problem has arisen. Changing the focus too late can make employees feel undervalued or hurt, leading to disengagement. Be proactive about promoting teamwork from the start.

### 2. Create Standard Operating Procedures (SOPs)

Implement clear and consistent Standard Operating Procedures (SOPs) across your team. When your staff understands that there are well-defined processes in place, they will realize that, while some particular staff may be favoured by a client, the salon's success doesn't rely on any one person. SOPs create a sense of equality and ensure that the business operates smoothly regardless of who is in charge of any particular task. This helps reinforce the idea that no staff member is indispensable. By this simple method, you make sure they understand that the brand is bigger than individuals.

### 3. Keep Your Options Open

It's essential to always keep preparing for the future. Regularly train new staff, even if you don't currently have a vacancy, so that you have a pool of trained individuals ready when needed. This approach not only ensures you have backups available, but it also sends a clear message to your current staff that while they are valued, they are not indispensable. If an employee begins to exhibit negative behaviour or attitudes, they will know that their position can be filled without any disruption in operations of the salon.

Over my decades of experience in the salon industry, I've witnessed owners struggling with difficult staff members who believe they are untouchable. In these situations, the owner often feels trapped, worried that firing the employee will disrupt the business. However, when they finally make the decision to let them go, they realize how much more peaceful the environment becomes within just a week or two. Clients adapt quickly, and the team often becomes more focused on growth and positive outcomes.

While it's essential to nurture a positive and supportive environment, it's equally important to avoid making any staff member feel indispensable. By appreciating the team as a whole, establishing clear SOPs, and always keeping your options open by training potential replacements, you create a balanced and thriving salon. This approach helps maintain a healthy atmosphere where everyone knows they are valued, but no one is above the system. Although it may seem challenging at first, embracing the idea that no one is irreplaceable or indispensable is a difficult but necessary step for the long-term success of your salon.

# CHAPTER 3

# TURNING PRODUCTS INTO PROFITS: RETAIL MAGIC

For a very long time, people with smaller salons have not considered the power of retail sales in salons, while in reality, retail sales play a crucial role in the salon industry, offering both economic and experiential value. Not only do retail products provide an additional revenue stream for salons, but they also enhance client satisfaction by allowing individuals to maintain their look and care regimen between visits. When stylists recommend products tailored to the client's specific needs, it reinforces the salon's authority and builds trust.

Furthermore, retail sales create opportunities for deeper engagement, helping salons stand out in a competitive market. Ultimately, the integration of retail into salon services elevates the overall client experience while supporting the long-term success of the business.

### 1. Sell the Right Product:

This is about understanding and recommending products based on the client's specific needs, not just trying to make a sale. One should analyse carefully before recommending any product to anyone. You show that you care about the quality of their skin or hair, and that your goal is to help maintain the benefits of the service you've provided. Remember that the advice should feel like aftercare, not a sales pitch. As pointed out in the above chapters, this builds trust and increases the likelihood that the client will return and listen to your future recommendations.

### 2. Client Education & Empowerment:

With knowledge available on their fingertips, clients are becoming more informed and selective. They appreciate it when you explain why a particular product is the best option for them based on their unique skin or hair concerns. This can be done, while you are performing a particular service and they are witnessing the results. Demonstrating how the product works during the service, how to use it at home, when to apply and per usage cost helps to push the product further to the "you need it" category. Letting the client feel the results (like softening skin after a manicure or smooth hair after a treatment), makes the recommendation more credible. You're not just talking, you're showing them the benefits firsthand.

### 3. Effective Communication:

Refine your words. Instead of simply saying "buy this," using phrases like "I recommend this for home" makes it feel more personal and less transactional. Also giving clients the per-use cost breakdown, such as "this shampoo will cost just Rs 10 per wash," instead of saying this shampoo is for Rs 1,000/- helps them see the product as an affordable investment in the results they're experiencing.

### 4. Sell but do not oversell

Offering options without pressuring the client is key. The recommendation should feel like a suggestion, not a demand. It is important to know when to start and when to stop. If the client doesn't purchase the product, don't let it impact your mood or interactions. I have seen people changing their tones and making expression, and thus the client feels she should buy, else the worker will get upset. But once they leave the salon, they promise themselves not to come back as they feel very uncomfortable. Keep the atmosphere positive and non-judgmental. If they don't buy now, they might return for the product later. So try selling, but overselling is a 100% no-no.

**5. Positive approach:**

The famous story of " let me add French fries with your burger", doubled the sales of a famous brand. So it's how positive you are. When the service is complete, you can smoothly transition to offering the product by simply asking, "let me get this billed with the service" This gives the client a chance to decide without feeling pressured. And the chances for her to say yes and more. The chances for the client buying is more than if you would have said " do you want to buy any product?" Then the answer is generally NO. The idea is to remain specific. Once you are sure of what to sell, they will surely buy.

If they decline, don't push it - just remain professional and friendly, keeping the door open for future opportunities. Simply say, " no worries, next time do buy it for the perfect result as shown."

By using this approach, you're creating a welcoming, professional, and trusting environment where clients feel cared for and valued, which is essential for long-term business growth in the salon industry.

## Let's Categorise The Products:

### 1. Necessary Aftercare for Long-Lasting Results:

While buying products for retail is a choice, in some cases it seems very important as it is the contention of the service done in the salon. For example, when you perform a service like a keratin treatment, you know that using the wrong products could undo the effects or cause the results to fade faster. Or when you have done a peel on the face, you want the client to use a particular face wash, night cream for healing and sunblock for the day for protection. Offering specialized products - such as SPF 50 sunblock cream or a sulphate-free shampoo recommended by the treatment brand - isn't just a sales tactic; it's a necessary step in maintaining the results you've delivered. Make sure you tell your client that it's not about selling more; it's about ensuring the longevity of the client's treatment and showing them that you genuinely care about their results. This also reinforces your expertise in the service you provided.

### 2. Enhance the Client's Experience:

On the other hand, there are those products which might not be essential for maintaining the service result, but they add value to the client's daily routine. For instance, offering a deodorant that makes them feel fresh or a body lotion that enhances their skin texture can make them feel pampered and cared for beyond just the service.

While these might not be "necessary," they still boost the client's confidence and well-being. Remember it is an important part of your role as a stylist or beautician. Products that make the client feel good - like a fragrance that reminds them of their experience at your salon - help create a positive association with your business.

### 3. Combination Products:

There are several retail products that are most effective when sold as a combination. For example, after providing a hair colour service to a client, recommending a set of colour-protecting products - such as a colour-save shampoo, colour-save hair mask, and a colour shine serum - can significantly improve the longevity of the results. This combination helps maintain the vibrancy and health of the coloured hair, reinforcing the value of the service.

When stylists recommend product bundles tailored to the client's specific treatment, it not only improves outcomes but also reinforces the salon's authority and builds trust. Clients are more likely to feel that their service was worth every penny when they see lasting results, and this leads to greater loyalty and word-of-mouth promotion. Ultimately, the integration of targeted retail combinations into salon services elevates the overall client experience while supporting the long-term success of the business.

### 4. Personalised Products:

There are few beauticians and hair specialist, who will personalise the regime and make the combination of the product for each client. I remember getting a similar experience from the Korean hair spa company, who modified their scalp care after analysing my scalp post the service taken and made the serum in front of me, keeping in mind the condition of my scalp. I am sure , if you do so, the client won't be able to switch to any other product ever. The key takeaway here is the approach: you're not pushing products on your clients. Instead, you're offering personalized recommendations and alternations, based on the individual needs and the services you've provided. When you explain how the product will enhance the result they've already seen, it's a natural extension of the service.

By framing product recommendations as part of the service, you're reinforcing the message that you care about your clients' long-term results, not just the immediate effect of the service. This approach helps deepen your relationship with clients and builds a foundation for loyalty, trust, and even referrals.

### 5. Seasonal & Festive Personalised Products:

Sell seasonally relevant products like Sunscreens in summer, body butters in winter. This will ensure effective sales along with making the client grab the product as a necessary item on the list. You may even try selling gift hampers during festive seasons (Diwali, Christmas, etc.) Place these items where they're visible and train staff to promote them accordingly - it boosts timely sales and makes your salon feel in tune with the client's current needs.

## Important Points To Consider While Selling Retail Products

### 1. Maintain Product Integrity

Never let discounts or schemes compromise your professional judgment. Recommend only what's right for the client's specific needs. Selling the wrong product — just for incentives — can hurt client trust and long-term relationships. Like I mentioned earlier, do not try to sell a comb to the bald man, sell him a hair treatment and gift him the comb, thereby also reflecting hope.

### 2. Be Transparent

If a product is part of a commission or discount scheme, be upfront. Clients appreciate honesty and will respect your transparency. It shows you're a professional, not just a salesperson. Everyone understands the pressure of targets, if your bonding is that strong with the client, you may share and make her feel happy in adding to your achievements. The feeling of "Queens crown each other" is there only in selected women, and you may see them becoming happy in purchasing the product to make you achieve your ultimate goal.

### 3. Avoid Over-Selling

The king rule, know when to start and know when to stop. It's about enhancing the client's experience, not overwhelming them. Over-selling feels pushy and creates discomfort. Focus on their actual needs—that builds credibility and loyalty.

### 4. Balance Retail with Service

Retail is a valuable add-on, not a replacement for excellent service. Don't let product-selling take away from your core strength: delivering amazing beauty services. It is important to avoid selling products that might reduce the frequency of client visits. For instance, it is appropriate to sell a night cream and facewash after a facial, but offering a complete skincare regime — such as a face wash, scrub, cream, and face pack — might lead clients to feel they can replicate the facial results at home. This could delay their next appointment as the Clients may believe that the products alone deliver the same benefits as a professional service, diminishing the perceived value of returning to the salon.

So be selective and strategic in your retail offerings. When done thoughtfully, retail can complement salon services, boost client satisfaction, and support business growth without undermining the demand for in-person treatments.

### 5. Select the Right Products

Stock products that reflect your salon's standards and brand values. Avoid crowding your shelves with random, off-brand items just because they're on discount. Clients notice these inconsistencies—and it can damage your image. The category of products you keep will reflect your personal choice and the knowledge you have about them. Thus carefully select them and place them in the right corner. It is just fine to have a selective, less crowded retail block than an overcrowded multiple choice option display.

### 6. Train Your Staff Thoroughly

Your team should be thoroughly aware of all aspects of a product:

- The USP of each product.
- Per-usage cost (helps in justifying pricing).
- How to introduce the product naturally during the service.
- How to avoid sounding like a sales pitch.

A confident, informed staff can create trust-based recommendations, not pressure-based sales.

As basic as it sounds, imagine, if they are selling a product and when the client asks any of the above details, they are either quiet or confused. This will be quiet embarrassing, and the client wont trust the staff again.

### 7. Exclusive Product Partnerships

Few brands sell exclusively through salons and maintain professional partnerships. These brands understand the importance of exclusivity, as it directly influences client retention and prevents them from turning to online retailers for reorders. Choosing retail brands that offer salon-only products is a smart strategy. Since clients can't find these products online or in regular stores, they are more likely to return to your salon for repurchasing. This naturally increases footfall and can drive additional service sales as well.

So be selective and strategic in your retail offerings. When done thoughtfully, retail sales can complement salon services, boost client satisfaction, and support business growth without undermining the demand for in-person treatments.

### 8. Choose Brands That Offer Training & Marketing Support

Work with companies that sell more than just products. These companies provide product trainings and make sure that the team is very well versed with their product range. They even give few personal benefits in achieving the sales goals and push the sales from their end. Such companies will also provide you with the marketing materials like posters, brochures outer facades, which adds on to the ambience of the salon.

### 9. Leverage Stories & Reels

Don't limit your social media to just service videos. Post about:

- New product arrivals
- Visible client results from using the after-care products
- Limited-time offers

Add a product reel with a discount mention, and you might attract new clients who were buying the same product from elsewhere. This adds visibility, engagement, and brand trust to your salon.

## Every Product Sold, Adds To The Economy Of The System

While you thought you are just selling a single product, let me show you that with a single sale, what actually happens in the background.

This is a brilliant breakdown of how selling a single product can have a cascading effect on the economy, and it highlights the far-reaching impact of retail sales, especially in the salon and beauty industry.

### 1. Selling a Product = Client's Result Maintained:

- When you sell the right product, you help the client maintain the results of the service they've received. This builds satisfaction and trust, ensuring the client sees the value in the treatment and the product.

### 2. Client's Result Maintained = Better Sales for the Salon:

- Clients who are happy with the results of their treatments and products are more likely to return for future services and products. This drives sales for the salon, creating a strong, loyal customer base.

### 3. Better Sales of the Salon = Incentives Met:

- As the salon's sales increase, employees (like stylists and beauticians) are likely to meet sales targets, earning incentives for their efforts. This motivates staff to provide better service and actively recommend products to clients.

### 4. Incentives Met = Better Salary for the Worker:

- Meeting sales targets and earning incentives directly leads to higher earnings for employees. This makes employees feel valued and helps boost their financial well-being.

### 5. Better Salary for the Worker = More Spending Power:

- With a better salary, workers are able to spend more on themselves and their families. This increases consumer spending in the economy, which helps drive demand for other goods and services.

**6. Better Retail Company Relationship = Better Discount by Retail Company:**

• As salons sell more products, they often establish stronger relationships with retail product suppliers. These relationships can lead to better deals, discounts, or even exclusive product offerings that benefit both the salon and its clients.

**7. Better Discounts by Retail Company = Their Targets Met:**

• The retail company supplying the products also benefits when salons meet sales targets, leading to increased product demand. When salons sell more, they can negotiate better terms with suppliers, benefiting from lower prices or larger product orders.

**8. Their Targets Met = Employees Getting Better Salaries:**

• When retail companies hit their sales goals, they can reinvest in their own employees, offering better compensation, bonuses, or improved working conditions, which further contributes to the local economy.

**9. These Employees Purchasing More Products = Adding to the Growth of Other Companies:**

• Increased demand for retail products means companies need to produce more, leading to more purchases from suppliers, creating a cycle of growth for manufacturers and distributors. This, in turn, benefits the overall market and fosters business expansion across industries.

**10. More Demand = More Employment:**

• As demand increases for both products and services, companies and salons will hire more workers, whether it's in manufacturing, distribution, or sales roles. This creates more jobs, which helps reduce unemployment rates.

**11. More Demand = More Research:**

• Growing demand encourages manufacturers to invest in research and development, leading to the creation of new, innovative products. This benefits consumers with better-quality goods and fuels a competitive market environment.

### 12. More Research = Better Products Getting Developed:

- As companies improve their research and development efforts, the market sees the emergence of higher-quality products that meet consumer needs more effectively. This constant cycle of improvement helps businesses stay relevant and competitive.

### 13. And This Cycle Continues:

- All of these effects are interrelated. The sale of one product sets off a ripple effect that contributes to the economy at multiple levels: individual, corporate, and national. By recommending the right product to a client, you're not only benefiting the salon or yourself, but you're also indirectly contributing to a much larger, more complex cycle of growth in the economy.

## The Bigger Picture:

Every sale, even something as simple as a shampoo or conditioner, contributes to a larger economic ecosystem. From job creation and business growth to innovation and national economic development, you, as a professional in the salon industry, are a part of something much bigger than just a service transaction. By recognizing the interconnectedness of these actions, you can see how vital your role is—not only in making the client happy but in contributing to the economy in meaningful ways.

# CHAPTER 4

# BUILDING STRONG PARTNERSHIPS: VENDOR MANAGEMENT

This is a chapter which will be extremely beneficial when it comes to the basic understanding of salon and vendor relationship. Vendors who supply products to each salon are the bridge between the brands and the end users, in this case, the salon. it is of utmost importance to understand the how this vendor relationship can be properly structured to derive maximum benefits.

## Structured Vendor Relationship

A structured vendor relationship refers to a strategic and organized approach to managing relationships with suppliers and vendors. It involves establishing clear expectations, terms, and communication channels to foster a mutually beneficial partnership. For example, a newly opened Indian salon is looking to establish a partnership with a vendor to procure hair care products. The salon aims to offer a wide range of high-quality products to cater to the diverse needs of its customers. However, the salon owner is unsure about the criteria to consider while selecting a vendor and wants to develop a structured purchasing plan to ensure a successful partnership. The salon needs to follow the process mentioned below as a guide book.

## 1. Techniques for Structuring a Vendor Relationship:

### a) Vendor Selection Criteria:

To effectively assess potential vendors, it is important to define specific criteria based on the salon's requirements and goals. Here is an Situation of how a salon can structure its vendor selection criteria:

| Vendor Selection Criteria | Weightage (Out of 10) |
|---|---|
| Product Quality | 8 |
| Pricing | 7 |
| Delivery Capabilities | 9 |
| Customer Service | 6 |
| Reputation | 8 |

**(Where 10 being the highest and 1 being the lowest)**

In this Situation, the salon assigns weightage to each criteria based on its importance. Product quality, delivery capabilities, and reputation hold higher weightage, indicating their significance in the decision-making process. The salon can rate potential vendors against these criteria and calculate a cumulative score to aid in vendor selection.

### b) Contractual Agreements:

A contractual agreement is a legally binding document between two or more parties that outlines the terms and conditions of their relationship, including the rights, obligations, and responsibilities of each party. It establishes a framework for the parties to fulfil their respective roles and ensures that both parties are aware of their rights and obligations. A contractual agreement typically includes details such as the scope of work, pricing and payment terms, delivery and lead times, quality control and assurance measures, termination conditions, and dispute resolution processes. It serves as a means to clarify expectations, protect the interests of all parties involved, and provide a basis for resolving any conflicts or disagreements that may arise during the course of the business relationship.

To structure the vendor relationship through contractual agreements, the following elements should be included:

- **Scope of Work:** Clearly define the products or services to be provided by the vendor. The list should be clear about both the demand and the supply to salon owner as well as the vendor.
- **Pricing and Payment Terms:** Specify the pricing structure, discounts, and payment terms agreed upon by both parties.

(**For Example**: The agreed-upon pricing will be as per the negotiated rates provided by XYZ Beauty Trader. Payment will be made within 30 days of product delivery.)

- **Delivery and Lead Times:** Outline expectations regarding product delivery, lead times, and any penalties for delays.

(**For example:** The vendor will deliver orders within 3-5 business days from the date of order confirmation. In case of any delays, he will provide prior notice and propose alternative delivery dates.

- **Quality Control and Assurance:** Establish guidelines for ensuring product quality, including inspections, certifications, and testing protocols.

(**For Example:** The Vendor ensures that all products meet industry standards and are compliant with relevant regulations. The salon has the right to conduct periodic inspections and request necessary certifications for quality assurance.)

- **Termination and Dispute Resolution:** Define conditions under which the contract can be terminated and the process for resolving disputes.

(**For Example:** Either party can terminate the contract with a 30-day notice period. In the case of any disputes, both parties agree to engage in mediation or arbitration to resolve the issue amicably.)

**c) Performance Metrics:**

Key performance indicators (KPIs) help monitor and evaluate the vendor's performance. Here are some Situational metrics that can be used:

- **On-time Delivery:** Measure the vendor's ability to deliver products within the agreed-upon timeframe.

- **Product Quality:** Assess the quality of products based on customer feedback, returns, or inspections.
- **Responsiveness:** Evaluate the vendor's promptness in addressing inquiries, concerns, and order modifications.
- **Order Accuracy:** Monitor the accuracy of product quantities, packaging, and specifications in delivered orders.

| Key Performance Indicators | Target | Actual Performance (Last Quarter) |
|---|---|---|
| On-time Delivery | 95% | 90% |
| Product Quality | 90% satisfaction rate | 80% satisfaction rate |
| Responsiveness | Respond to inquiries within 24 hours | Average response time: 12 hours |
| Order Accuracy | 99% accuracy | 90% accuracy |

In this Situation, the salon sets specific targets for each performance metric and tracks the vendor's actual performance over a designated period. Any gaps between the targets and actual performance can be addressed through performance improvement discussions with the vendor.

By structuring the vendor relationship with defined selection criteria, contractual agreements, and performance metrics, the salon can establish a strong partnership with reliable vendors and ensure smooth procurement processes.

### 2. Developing a Purchasing Plan:

A purchasing plan is a strategic document that outlines the salon's approach to procuring retail products from vendors. It helps ensure efficient and effective purchasing processes while aligning with the salon's goals and objectives. Here's an Situation of how to develop a purchasing plan:

#### a) Assessing Demand and Inventory Needs:

To develop a purchasing plan, the salon needs to assess its demand for retail products and determine the inventory needs. This can be done by analysing historical sales data, understanding seasonal trends, and considering upcoming promotions or events. By understanding the demand patterns, the salon can make informed decisions regarding inventory levels and purchasing quantities.

**For Example:** A Salon analysed its sales data for the past year and identified a seasonal spike in demand for hair care products during the summer months. They also noticed increased sales during festivals and holiday seasons. Based on this analysis, they anticipate a 20% increase in hair care product sales during the summer and a 15% increase during festivals and holiday periods. So now, based on data, when they are clear on the demand variation, they will order accordingly to have sufficient inventory levels.

### b) Setting Budget and Financial Considerations:

The purchasing plan should incorporate budgeting and financial considerations. The salon needs to determine the budget allocated for purchasing retail products and set spending limits for each product category.

This ensures that purchasing activities are aligned with the salon's financial capabilities.

**For example:** A budget allocation can be like:

- Hair care Products: INR 50,000
- Skincare Products: INR 30,000
- Nail Care Products: INR 20,000
- Makeup Products: INR 15,000

This budget allocation will certainly change time to time depending on the sales.

### c) Identifying Preferred Vendors:

The purchasing plan should identify and prioritize preferred vendors based on factors such as product quality, pricing, reliability, time taken for delivery and customer service. This helps streamline the procurement process and build stronger relationships with key vendors.

### d) Establishing Order Frequency and Lead Times:

The purchasing plan should determine the frequency of placing orders and the lead times required by vendors for product delivery. This ensures that the salon maintains adequate inventory levels while avoiding stock outs or excessive inventory.

**Order Frequency and Lead Times:**

- Hair care Products: Order bi-weekly with a lead time of 3 days.
- Skincare Products: Order monthly with a lead time of 5 days.
- Nail Care Products: Order quarterly with a lead time of 7 days.
- Makeup Products: Order as needed with a lead time of 2 days.

**e) Reviewing and Updating the Plan:**

The purchasing plan should be reviewed periodically to assess its effectiveness and make necessary adjustments. This includes analysing sales data, vendor performance, market trends, and customer feedback. The plan should be updated to reflect any changes in demand patterns, budget constraints, or vendor relationships.

By developing a comprehensive purchasing plan, a salon can ensure that it procures retail products strategically, meets customer demand efficiently, optimizes inventory levels, and maintains a healthy vendor relationship.

### 3. Evaluating Vendors:

**a) Product Quality and Compliance:** Assess vendors based on the quality and compliance of their products with industry standards and regulations.

**b) Reliability and Delivery Performance:** Evaluate the vendor's track record for timely and accurate deliveries to ensure a steady supply of products, within the stipulated timelines.

**c) Reputation and Customer Feedback:** Consider the vendor's reputation in the market and gather customer feedback to assess their credibility and satisfaction levels.

**Table: Vendor Evaluation Criteria**

| Criteria | Description |
|---|---|
| Product Quality | Evaluate the quality and effectiveness of the vendor's products. |
| Pricing | Compare pricing options to ensure competitive and reasonable rates. |
| Delivery Performance | Assess the vendor's track record for on-time and accurate deliveries. |
| Customer Service | Evaluate the vendor's responsiveness and ability to address issues. |
| Reliability | Consider the vendor's reliability in terms of product availability. |
| Reputation | Assess the vendor's reputation and credibility in the market. |

**4. Negotiating with Vendors:** Negotiating with vendors is an important aspect of vendor management in the salon industry. Effective negotiation techniques and strategies can help salon owners secure favourable pricing, terms, and conditions, and establish long-term partnerships with vendors. Here are some key elements to consider when negotiating with vendors:

**a) Price Negotiation:** Price negotiation involves engaging in discussions and bargaining with vendors to secure the best possible pricing for products or services. Salon owners can leverage their purchasing power, market knowledge, and competitive offers to negotiate lower prices, volume discounts, or special promotional pricing. By effectively negotiating prices, salon owners can optimize their purchasing costs and improve their profit margins.

During price negotiations, a salon owner may request a lower per-unit price for a bulk order of hair care products, citing their consistent and substantial purchasing volume. The vendor may be willing to provide a discounted price to maintain the salon's business and secure a long-term partnership.

**b) Terms and Conditions:** Negotiating favourable terms and conditions is crucial to protect the salon's interests and ensure a smooth vendor relationship. This includes discussing and agreeing upon payment terms, return policies, warranties, and any other contractual obligations. Salon owners should carefully review and negotiate these terms to minimize risks and address specific needs or concerns.

During negotiations, a salon owner may negotiate extended payment terms with a vendor, such as a 60-day payment window instead of the standard 30 days. This provides the salon with more flexibility in managing cash flow and aligns with their specific financial requirements.

**c) Long-term Partnerships:** Building long-term partnerships with vendors can offer numerous benefits for both parties. Establishing mutually beneficial relationships based on trust, open communication, and shared business objectives can lead to more favourable terms, exclusive offers, and collaborative growth opportunities.

In negotiations, a salon owner may express their interest in a long-term partnership with a specific vendor. They can discuss the potential for increased business volumes, joint marketing efforts, or exclusive access to new product launches. By highlighting the advantages of a long-term partnership, the salon owner can negotiate more favourable terms and establish a strategic alliance that benefits both parties.

Negotiating with vendors requires effective communication, preparation, and a clear understanding of the salon's needs and objectives. It is important for salon owners to approach negotiations with a win-win mindset, seeking to find mutually beneficial solutions that support the growth and success of both the salon and the vendor.

# CHAPTER 5

# OOPS MOMENTS: DEALING WITH AN UPSET CLIENT

Satisfactorily handling a complaining client in a salon is crucial for maintaining a positive reputation and ensuring long-term customer loyalty. It's important to address the issue promptly, professionally, and empathetically.

This is one of my favourite topics. I have seen people running away from an unsatisfied client, thereby exacerbating the situation. Somehow, where ever I have worked or whichever department I am into, I have always found myself pushed to the forefront to handle them. Indeed, everyone believes that I will definitely resolve the issue, thus, I just love this. The trick is easy. Here's a step-by-step guide on how to manage the situation effectively, while ensuring that both the client and the staff feel respected and heard.

**o Don't be scared**

This is the most important thing to remember. The client came to get a service done. Somehow a misunderstanding happened in terms of the result expected and the result achieved. Now she is unsatisfied and wants someone to listen, understand and give her a solution. This is not the time to hide behind doors and avoid her. Now comes the time to display those management skills and make sure that all the necessary steps are taken, so that the client leaves the premises satisfied and happy. So, don't be scared, just follow the steps and sort it out easily.

**o Take the client to a quiet room**

There are chances that the client would start the complaint either on the workstation, or at the reception. They might ask for the manager or simply start getting furious on the staff responsible. It is important that at that very moment, you take her to a closed cabin. The cabin should be closed one, so that no noise can be heard by the other clients, as they might get influenced and carry a bad impression. Make sure the room has a cool temperature, and sitting arrangement, so that the client is comfortable. Make sure she sits and is in relaxed posisiton.

**o Serve her water**

This is also important, so much so that I had to make a separate point of it. I have practised it, and you will be surprised, when you drink water, and pause for few minutes, half of your anger mellows down. Have you ever tried it? I have and it always works. So, serve her water and tell her to stay calm. Assure her that you will listen to the details and will make sure her problem is resolved. This will make the whole restlessness reduce.

**Now comes the main step:**

**o Listen Attentively and Stay Calm**

- **Listen without Interrupting:**

Let the client speak fully without interrupting, so they feel heard and understood. Don't get defensive or make excuses. Do not, and make sure you do not, make any negative facial expressions. Just nod your head and do not smile either. Keep a calm face and listen attentively.

- **Empathize:** Acknowledge their feelings. Say something like, "I understand how frustrating that must be for you," or "I'm so sorry that you had this experience." Sometimes, just being a good listener and showing genuine concern can diffuse a lot of tension. Make sure she knows that you feel her problem and are ready to solve it.

## o Apologize Sincerely

• A genuine apology is essential, even if the staff might not have intentionally made a mistake. For example, "I'm really sorry you didn't have the experience you were expecting, and I'll do everything I can to make it right."

• **Avoid saying:**

"I'm sorry you feel that way," as this can sound dismissive. Instead, take responsibility for the salon's service, regardless of the cause. Be very careful of the words you choose. Do not blame the staff, saying "she is like this only, or we have so many complaints of her."

Never use the term "I will give you a better staff next time". Be very careful that you don't blame the staff at this point. You are sorry that it happened, but not playing any blame game or politics in the team, rather taking the responsibility of the incident that has taken place. So, choose your words carefully.

## o Find a Solution or Offer Compensation

• Politely ask, "What can I do to make this right for you?" This makes the client feel in control and ensures that you're offering a solution that they find satisfactory. Once she tells you how she feels about it, tell her to wait in the same room. Discuss the problem with the staff and work out the solution. Try to take less time , don't keep the client waiting.

**The solution can be as simple as:**

• Staff apologising and saying "ma'am I am so sorry, I have been serving for so many years, this won't happen again."

• You giving her an option of same service free during her next visit, so that you are sure she will revisit.

• In case it's a fixable mistake (e.g., incorrect makeup application or hair colour), offer to correct it on the spot, if possible. This will use a little bit of uncalculated time, but it will satisfy her for sure.

• Last and only as a last resort, if the complaint is about a service or product, consider offering a partial refund. Alternatively, offer a complimentary service or upgrade on their next visit. For example: "As a gesture of goodwill, we would be happy to offer you a complimentary hair treatment or a discount on your next service."

### o Maintain Professionalism and Stay Calm

• Control the Situation: Always remain professional, calm, and polite, no matter how upset the client is. Don't let emotions take over.

• Avoid Blaming Staff in Front of Clients: Do not criticize or blame staff members in front of the client. It can make the situation worse and harm team morale.

### o Follow-Up After the Visit

• After resolving the issue, follow up with the client via phone or WhatsApp message to ensure they are satisfied with the resolution and offer them another chance to provide feedback.

• In addition send them a thank you note or offer them a discount on their next service as a goodwill gesture to show you value their business.

• This follow-up can turn a dissatisfied customer into a loyal one and shows you genuinely care about their satisfaction.

Once the client has gone and you have won brownie points by making her happy, there is another crucial aspect to handle.

## How to Balance the Staff who has made the mistake:

The client is now happy, but the staff might be disappointed. He might feel that it was not his mistake, or the client has blamed him wrongly, and you as the manager, have also taken the client's side. Make sure you follow the steps given below to obviate chances of creating an unsatisfied staff and thereby raising even a bigger issue of retention.

### 1. Maintain Fairness

- Once the client is satisfied, address the issue with the staff involved in a private, non-confrontational manner. Make sure you listen to the staff with equal importance and patience as you gave the client. Remember, the staff at this point will behave like the warrior who has lost a battle and may get furious about the client, or the additional discount given, and thinks that she has caused a loss to the company. She might be either angry or super upset because of her actions and the episode that has taken place. So same steps, take her to a calm place, and yes, serve her water too. Then listen to her side.

- Once you have heard and analysed the issue, instead of blaming the staff, focus on the root cause of the issue. Make the staff understand her mistake. This is important to prevent it from happening in the future. For example, "Let's review the steps we can take to improve communication with clients about their expectations. The client came for a relaxing facial, and we gave her the room where there was constant noise of the staff, eating lunch in the pantry. The whole air was filled with lunch and the other staff members kept on coming in the room to ask you to join for the lunch. I understand and value, that you delayed your break and kept on doing the service, but the client felt that you are in a hurry and also could not relax with those noises. So let us make sure that from the next time, we avoid the room near the pantry during lunch and tea hours. Also, I will take a meeting tomorrow and will remind everyone not to enter the facial rooms while the client is getting the service done. This will make the clients experience a relaxing service and we would not have any more complaints on this topic". See how simple this was, as compared to shouting at the staff saying things like, "Why were you all talking while eating, and I am sure you finished all her steps in lesser time, so that you could join your friends who were waiting for the lunch". How you handle the situation with your staff is also very important. The art is to use the complaint as a learning opportunity for everyone involved.

## 2. Provide Clear Feedback to Staff

- It is important that you sit down with the staff member(s) involved and discuss the complaint. Ensure the staff member understands what went wrong without making them feel attacked. Let them tell you the solution, and you will be surprised that since the suggestion came from them, they will follow it. This will be more impactful, than you telling them the solution and asking them to follow the rule, set by you.

- Clarify the standards and procedures they need to follow to prevent similar comp.laints. If it's a recurring issue, provide additional training or refreshers.

o **For example:** "In this situation, the client expected a specific colour, and the miscommunication led to disappointment. Let's ensure we double-check the client's preferences next time. Let us do the strand test and then confirm the results."

## 3. Empower Staff with the Tools to Handle Complaints

- Analyse carefully why the complaint arose in the first place. If the complaint was because of the lack of proper training, then act accordingly. Provide training to your staff on the skill and also on soft skills. It is important that they know how to bring the results promised and also how to handle customer complaints professionally, including active listening, problem-solving, and remaining calm under pressure.

- Empower your team to resolve minor issues on the spot without always having to escalate to every issue to the management. This reduces friction and makes the client feel valued immediately. This also makes the bonding of the team stronger. Empowering staff gives them confidence to handle complaints and take ownership of their actions, leading to better customer service in the long run.

## 4. Create a Positive Team Culture

- Foster an environment where the staff feels supported rather than blamed. When mistakes happen, the focus should be on learning and improvement, not punishment. Be very careful about not taking any sides and being totally non partial at this time, otherwise the whole activity will be of no use.

- Promote a culture where staff work together to solve client issues, rather than letting any one individual carry the burden alone. When staff members feel supported, they are more likely to be proactive and empathetic while handling future complaints.

- Make sure you celebrate the fact that the client was satisfied with the resolution. Share positive feedback on how staff members handled the situation to encourage best practices.
- The mantra is " scold in private, appreciate in public" for every action always.

# CHAPTER 6

# WHO'S WATCHING? THE POWER OF MYSTERY SHOPPING

"N" number of times, I've heard salon owners say, "I can't travel, Gunjann—how can I leave my salon behind?" It's rarely about money or even time. The real reason? Fear.

Fear of not knowing what happens behind their back—how staff will behave with clients, how services will be delivered, or whether the integrity of their brand will be upheld in their absence.

But here's the truth: You'll never know unless you test it.

Do you really want to know what happens when you're not around? Not just through your CCTV cameras—but from the eyes of the client who walks in unsuspectingly?

That's where mystery shoppers come in.

I once sent someone to a salon, while the owner was having lunch with me. The auditor was told to do the following things:

- Create a drama of being unsatisfied, at the front desk before payment.

• Ask for multiple discounts and free add-ons.

• Try bribing a therapist in the waxing room to "do an extra job" for just a tip.

The findings were eye-opening—and not all negative. It helped the salon owner realize:

• Why some first-time clients never returned—even though they smiled when they left.

• Which team members were loyal, professional, and respectful even under pressure.

• Who saw an opportunity to bend the rules when no one was "watching".

These experiences can be confronting—but they're also liberating.

Because once you know the truth, you can fix it.

You can train better, reward loyalty, and finally plan that trip you've been putting off for years—knowing your brand is safe, even when you're away.

## Choosing the Right Auditor

The success of a mystery shopping audit hinges on choosing the right auditor. This is crucial for obtaining accurate, actionable insights about your salon's customer experience. The auditor will evaluate several facets of your services, from customer service and product knowledge to cleanliness and staff professionalism.

In some cases, you may need to focus on specific concerns—such as whether a makeup artist gives out her personal contact number and agrees to work with clients outside of the salon as a freelancer. If that's the case, ensure your auditor is briefed on such unique situations for an in-depth evaluation.

## How to Choose the Right Auditor:

**1. Clarify Your Objectives:** Before you select an auditor, it's vital to know what you want to assess. Your audit should be honest, transparent, and thorough—nothing should be left out. For example, you may need to review aspects like:

o Customer service.

o Staff professionalism.

o Cleanliness.

o Product knowledge.

o Specific behaviour or incidents, such as unauthorized personal interactions between staff and clients.

**2. Key Traits to Look for in an Auditor:**

o **No Previous Visits:** Ensure the auditor has never been to your salon before, so their experience will be unbiased.

o **Attention to Detail:** The auditor should be excellent at observing small details, like cleanliness, service timing, and even subtle staff interactions.

o **Experience of the Industry:** It's beneficial if the auditor has had their services done at other competitive salons to compare the experience.

o **Truthfulness:** Choose someone who isn't afraid to tell you the honest truth, even if it's uncomfortable.

o **Professionalism:** The auditor must approach the task with seriousness and professionalism. They should appear neutral and not raise suspicion among your staff.

o **Objectivity:** Ensure they evaluate based on facts, not personal preferences or biases.

o **Confidentiality:** The auditor should understand the importance of confidentiality to protect your staff's integrity and to ensure accurate feedback. She should not talk about this to any other person/salon post her work and reporting is over.

o **Unobtrusiveness:** The auditor must blend in naturally and not seem like someone "reporting" on every little thing. Their observations should feel like those of a regular client.

**3. Third-Party Audit Companies:** If you're working with a mystery shopping agency, be sure to check their references and reviews. Ask for examples of their previous work and inquire about their success rate in delivering valuable feedback. Agencies often have experience with multiple salons, which can bring a broader perspective on your service quality compared to a single auditor.

## Know the End Result You Want from the Audit

Before you engage the auditor, it's crucial to know exactly what you want to assess. A detailed and thorough audit will provide valuable insights into your salon's performance. Meeting with the auditor in advance and clearly communicating your objectives is essential to ensure that they focus on the right aspects.

## Important Considerations:

- Avoid influencing the auditor's perception by mentioning anything specific about the salon. I would suggest telling the auditor: "Search for my salon, ABC, on Google, find the address, book an appointment by phone, follow the map, and arrive without knowing the location in advance."

By doing this, the auditor remains unbiased and assesses your salon the same way a regular client would.

## Areas to Focus on During the Audit:

### 1. Customer Service:

o How does the team behave when you're not there?

o Are they responsive to client inquiries, or does it take too long to reach someone (e.g., via phone or Google Maps)?

o Do they provide consistent, friendly service to all clients?

o Do they value the importance that you have taken an appointment and thus you should wait the least for the services?

### 2. Service Quality:

o Does the team deliver services with the same level of excellence when you're not around?

o Are clients satisfied with the quality of their treatments?

o What are other clients(if any) reaction, who are paying the bill while the auditor was waiting of her service to start.

### 3. Up-Selling and Cross-Selling:

o Does the staff recommend services or products without being pushy?

o How well do they introduce clients to additional services (e.g., aftercare products, add-ons)?

o Is there a balance between making a sale and maintaining a friendly, client-first approach?

### 4. Ambiance and Cleanliness:

o What is the vibe or aura of the salon? Does it feel welcoming and clean?

o How does the salon smell? Is it fresh and pleasant?

o How was the music? Both the volume and the type.

o Was the washroom clan?

o Was the salon smelling of food post meal time?

o Does the ambiance match the professionalism of your brand?

**5. Staff Professionalism:**

o Do they maintain professionalism, even when you are not there?

o Are they respectful to each other and to the clients?

o How do they handle complaints or issues that arise?

o Are they maintaining required standards of oral and body hygiene?

## Specific Points to Investigate:

If you have specific concerns or suspicions, ensure that the auditor is aware and can look for these during their visit:

**1. Staff Behaviour:**

o Do they give out their personal numbers or offer home services at a lower cost?

o How do they react if they're asked about the owner or the business? Are there negative comments or gossip?

o Do they try to subtly ask for tips or mention financial difficulties?

**2. Team Dynamics:**

o How does the staff interact with each other?

o Are they respectful, or is there back-biting or gossiping about management or other team members?

o How do they react to job offers?

**3. Sales Ethics:**

o Does the staff refuses services when it's near closing hours?

o Do they start blaming each other or create drama if a client complains?

**4. Client Retention:**

o How well does the team handle an unsatisfied client?

o Are they able to resolve issues effectively?

o Does the manager ensure that clients are satisfied and encourage them to return

o Do they ask for the google review or push to post a positive review only?

## The Final Question:

After all is said and done, always ask the final question to truly assess the client's experience:

"If you had the money, would you come back to this salon for the same service?"

o Yes, why?

o No, why not?

This will provide you with final, unfiltered insights into what needs to be improved and what aspects of your salon are working well.

By taking a deep, non-biased look at your salon through this audit, you will gain a true picture of its strengths and weaknesses. It's essential to be transparent with the auditor, ensuring they understand the value of an honest and thorough assessment.

1. It can be a simple reason that you want to see how the team behaves once you are not there?
2. Why a client calls but is unable to reach by google map?
3. Once the client reaches, what is the vibe she is getting?
4. What does the salon aura say: positive or confused?
5. Is the manager good enough to attend to her needs?
6. Does the salon smell fresh?
7. Do they behave very casually when they know the owner is not there?
8. How does she rate the 5 senses of Salon Aura: cleanliness, positivity, smiles of team present, music, the water or refreshments served?
9. Do they call back to ask for next appointment once the client leaves?
10. Most important, does the team know, when to start and when to stop in pitching for sale of services and products.

If you are suspicious of any activity, make sure the auditor knows about it in advance and she can ask the question as a client who is visiting the salon, when the owner is not there.

1. Check if the staff give their number.

2. If they agree to do home services at lesser cost.

3. If the staff talks negatively about the owner, once you ask them.

4. Do they ask for tips by telling indirectly how they are underpaid and require more money.

5. How do they react when you offer them a job in a nearby salon with just ₹ 500/1000 extra.

6. Do they respect each other or talk behind the back of their manager and any team member to become more friendly.

7. Do they recommend a new service, even when they know that it is almost closing time?

8. Do they start blaming each other if you complain?

9. Has the team become one and handles an unsatisfied client as a team?

10. How does the manager react once they find that you won't pay as you have a gift voucher which you won in the game somewhere last week?

## Repeat Regularly

One audit might open your eyes to several aspects of your salon's performance, but one survey is never enough. To truly measure progress and maintain high standards, regular mystery shopping is essential. This will help track improvements, highlight inconsistencies, and ensure that your staff continues to provide excellent service.

## Decide on the Frequency:

- **One-time Evaluation:** This is perfect for gauging the initial client experience and identifying immediate issues.
- **Regular Audits:** Ongoing mystery shopping allows you to track improvements over time, uncover hidden issues, and ensure that the quality of service remains consistent or even improves.

## Key Guidelines for Regular Audits:

- **Fresh Auditors:** It's important to appoint a new auditor each time. This ensures that the feedback remains unbiased and fresh. They should be fully aligned with your desired quality of evaluation.

- **Consistent Frequency:** Set a consistent schedule for evaluations. For example, conducting audits monthly or quarterly will give you regular insights into your salon's performance. You'll be able to spot patterns and make timely adjustments.

By repeating these audits regularly, you ensure that your salon doesn't just meet standards once but continues to improve and evolve to stay ahead of the competition.

## Discuss the Audit and Take Action

Once the audit is complete, it is essential to discuss the findings of the Audit with your team. This ensures that everyone is aligned and understands where improvements are needed or where the team is excelling.

**Here's how you can handle the results effectively:**

### Positive Audit Results:

- **Celebrate the Success:** If the audit shows a positive result, wait for a week to let it sink in. Then, gather the team and mention that an audit was conducted last week (without revealing the auditor's identity).

- **Acknowledge their Efforts:** Express how pleased you are with the outcome and how proud you are of their performance.

- **Reward the Team:** Celebrate the success with a team reward like a movie night together or a staff lunch outside. This not only boosts morale but also reinforces the idea that great performance will be recognized and rewarded.

### Negative Audit Results:

- **Hold an Important Meeting:** If the audit results are negative, address it immediately in a meeting with the staff. Be transparent about the issues the audit uncovered and the areas that need improvement.

- **Action Plan for Improvement:** Discuss actionable steps to rectify the problems. This could range from encouraging staff to pay more attention to detail to making tough decisions like removing a staff member if necessary.

- **Be Open and Clear:** Make it clear that the audit serves as a lesson for the whole team, emphasizing that the company is always monitoring the quality of service, even when you're away. This will help bringing discipline and a sense of responsibility in the staff.

## Key Actionable Steps:

**1. Assess Performance Across Multiple Criteria:** Look at various factors such as customer service, professionalism, product knowledge, and cleanliness to gain a comprehensive view of the client experience.

**2. Provide Feedback:** Share the results of the audit with the staff, making sure to keep the identity of the auditor confidential. Use this feedback as a training opportunity for improvement. Don't make it should like a complaint or sarcasm activity. Else every regular client will be mistaken as an auditor and the team won't be comfortable with the environment.

**3. Take Corrective Action:** Where weaknesses are identified, implement strategies to address them. This might involve additional training, role-playing, or coaching on handling specific situations. If corrective action is not taken, the whole purpose will get defeated. If needed to remove a staff member, do it. I know this sounds difficult, as she might be your favourite employee, but remember that she will cause more harm in the system, than being out. So, take that difficult yet important step and go ahead.

**4. Encourage Continuous Improvement:** The ultimate goal is to keep improving the customer experience and team performance. Use feedback analysis to coach and develop your staff, helping them become better at what they do.

**5. Create a Transparent Culture:** Ensure that feedback is valued, whether from mystery shoppers, clients, or peers. Sometimes the result of the audit is so bitter or surprising that we don't want to agree with them. But take this with a pill. Encourage an environment where your team feels comfortable discussing challenges they face and how they can improve.

**6. Ongoing Training:** Ensure that staff engages in continuous training and personal development. This not only improves service but also boosts staff morale and retention.

By approaching the audit process this way, you can ensure that it's not just about checking off boxes but about creating a continuous feedback loop for improvement and fostering a high-performing team that understands the importance of customer satisfaction.

# CHAPTER 7

# A SALON REVOLUTION: ARTIFICIAL INTELLIGENCE & YOU:

It is said, "AI won't steal the jobs of the people, the people who are adept at using AI will take the jobs of those who are not!". Whether that is true or not may be debated, but one thing is a certainty, the arrival of AI is like the computer revolution, it is here to stay. So, where's the harm in updating oneself?

During my visit to Assam for an exhibition, I met a fascinating gentleman "Akshay Poorey" over lunch who completely changed how I viewed salon software. Until that day, I, like many others, thought of software as something meant only for billing and appointments. But, that day over lunch, before dessert arrived, I had already promised him that my next book would carry a chapter on how AI and software tools are transforming the beauty industry.

He listed n number of advantages of integrating smart software into salon operations. I'm listing the top five that, in my opinion, can help a salon evolve into a brand, not just remain the salon-next-door—and help you double your profits, not just your sales.

## Data and Records at Your Fingertips

Client data is the true legacy of any salon. The way you preserve and use it speaks volumes about your professionalism and your potential for growth.

### Why it matters:

• Detailed client records enhance customer satisfaction by helping personalize every experience. I clearly remember when we did not use a software, but surely collected the data. Based on this, when we called, it used to irritate the client, the usual refrain being that last time also we asked the same things, why are we repeating the same questions. Even we used to be clueless about putting this available data to a better use than just calling the client.

• It ensures regulatory compliance, especially for professional liability coverage. In many cases, you must retain treatment details for at least seven years—and missing this can void your insurance. And this comes so handy when the client appears from nowhere saying that her few sittings are pending and you can't find any trace of that record.

• Storing this data manually is risky. A robust salon software can automate and securely manage all this information. Indeed a file getting stolen, or just damaged will make you lose the entire history of hundreds of clients. With software, it is safe in cloud or a backup is always handy with the creaters.

• **The real use comes when you can save various details about the clients like :**

o Treatment history

o Product usage and preferences

o Allergies or skin sensitivities

o Frequency of visits

o Feedback and complaints

o Missed appointments

o Upcoming birthdays

o Even their preferred beverage!

• Imagine the experience when a client is greeted with, "Would you like your usual green tea while we prep your treatment?" Or the hair therapist is told "be careful, ma'am is allergic to ammonia-based hair colour, so use the non-ammonia series". With these small, yet useful details, you can simply win the heart of the client. They will feel like family, and would willingly adjust to any minor negligence, if it occurs.

• The data also shows, the pattern of the client. The kind of services she has opted for, and the others which she can be recommended. Imagine a client who is regular for facial at your salon, if shortlisted and given a discount on head massage? I am sure they would love to try that too and might even become regular in the hair section of the salon.

• We all are aware of the reminder calls, which we do to call our clients for services, after a month, if they have not visited in the interim. But with this you may also filter them to the details of product reorders. If they have taken a face serums 2 months back and it was just 30 ml, then it would be appropriate to remind the client to stock it up too.

• Another detail which call be pulled out, is about the clients who opt for services only during "sales". So, once you are planning any sale, or happy hours in the salon, these clients can be reached exclusively, as you are sure that they will visit the moment they are informed about a sale.

• As an owner you can even glance through the data of what services you are getting major complaints about. And then dive deeper. Is it about the service performer or the wrong product? This will solve the problem and the required corrections can be made, either by retraining the staff or changing the product.

## Smart Feedback Filtering: How AI Saves Your Salon's Reputation

Nowadays, if we have to book a salon for service, buy a beauty product or opt for a freelancer for a home service, we just google the reviews posted by clients. On the same note as a brand owner we all worry about is how to handle negative Google reviews. Just one low rating can damage the image you've worked so hard to build. But what if I told you that AI can now act as a smart filter, letting you catch and resolve negative feedback before it goes public?

That's exactly what advanced salon software now offers—intelligent sentiment handling built into the feedback system.

### This Is How It Works:

When a client submits feedback—via form, chatbot, or SMS—the system uses Natural Language Processing (NLP) to analyse the sentiment of the feedback.

### If the Feedback is Positive:

**Example:** "Loved my facial! The beauty therapist was amazing!"

- The system thanks the client automatically.
- It then sends a link encouraging them to leave a review on Google or other platforms.
- This ensures more good reviews online, building your reputation organically.

### If the Feedback is Negative or Neutral:

**Example:** "The service was delayed" or "Not happy with my hair colour."

- The system flags the feedback internally.
- It prevents the review from being posted directly to Google.

- **The AI instantly:**

o Notifies the salon manager or complaint resolution team

o Creates a support ticket

o Sends an automatic message like:

"We're sorry to hear that. A manager will contact you shortly to resolve the issue."

o Thus, the review is not posted online.

**This Gives You a Second Chance:**

This small but powerful feature gives you a second chance. Many times, clients are genuinely upset but open to a resolution. A quick follow-up call, a redo service, or even a simple apology can turn the situation around.

Once resolved, you can politely ask the client to share their updated experience on Google. At that point, the feedback is likely to be not just neutral—but glowing.

By handling the issue in-house, you're avoiding public damage and showing the client that you genuinely care more about their experience than just the review score.

Now imagine the same scenario, without AI, which is the case of many salons till date. The client visits, gets the service done. Doesn't complain there and leaves quietly. Reaches home and decides to post something negative online. Now you are busy in day-to-day routine and miss out on the complaint posted. You will lose many clients, who read the complaint online as a negative review. You will also surely loose this client forever and she will be deeply hurt by the fact that her complaint was not taken seriously. To cap it, the client will talk about the experience in her group, about her being unsatisfied and being more upset that no one cared to revert to her after she posted the complaint. This is likely to spread like fire and thus gain a negative PR, which you would have sorted with just a phone call with the help of getting it flagged & pulled out by AI.

Whatever other uses you may put AI to, this is the single most important reason to install a software in your firm today itself!

## Booking Appointments Through Your Website — A True Game Changer

Mark my words—it is a **game changer.**

Picture this: a bride-to-be is hunting online for a makeup artist for her big day. She Googles, and your salon's website appears right at the top.

She clicks—and what she finds is a dull, static page with a contact number tucked at the bottom. Do you think, she will scroll down, remember the number, dial on the phone, and wait for the salon receptionist to answer the phone?

**Instead, imagine that she sees:**

- A webpage full of Stunning visuals of your work.
- Before-and-after transformations.
- Real client feedback.
- A pop-up asking if she'd like to book an appointment right now?
- The moment she clicks yes, the number getting flashed in the mobile and the system of the salon.
- An appointment is generated in the appointment sheet of the salon.
- She getting an automatic reminder of her appointment a day prior and an hour prior to the date and time too.
- All this automatically managed by the system.

I am sure you would agree that with the above steps, the client won't forget the appointment. She will know how much you value a lead and will find you more professional without even stepping into the salon. It's not just a website. It's your 24/7 digital front desk, and it's about to book your next high-ticket client.

### How AI Makes It Happen:

#### 1. AI Chatbot Integration

- As soon as someone lands on your site, a chatbot gently prompts:

"Hi there! Would you like help booking your appointment?"

• The bot guides the visitor step by step:

o What service are you looking for? (e.g., bridal makeup, pre-bridal package, grooming session)

o What day/time works best for you?

## 2. Real-Time Scheduling

• The AI chatbot pulls up your team's availability in real-time.

• It offers available slots and even schedules a free trial, if needed.

• It can highlight ongoing offers or bridal packages, making the booking more appealing.

## 3. Instant Confirmation & Reminders

• Once confirmed, the system:

o Sends a booking confirmation immediately

o Automatically schedules reminder messages a few days and hours before the appointment—reducing no-shows

## 4. Easy Payments & Cancellations

• Clients can pay online at the time of booking—one less thing to worry about.

• Need to reschedule? No problem.

o The chatbot can handle rescheduling or cancellations instantly and updates your salon's dashboard too.

## Now Compare That to a 'Contact Us' Button at the bottom of the website...

Let's be honest. A traditional site with a "Contact Us" form or phone number can't compete with this level of service. While you're waiting for a call or a DM, the AI-powered site has already booked the client, confirmed the service, and sent out a reminder—all without a single human involved.

That's not just automation. That's professionalism upscaled manyfold.

## Salary Calculation Made Easy with AI

As we always say: "Happy staff = Happier clients."

But imagine this—your team works hard all month, only to receive a miscalculated salary. Even if it's unintentional, it can break trust instantly. And unfortunately, the blame doesn't stop at HR or accounts—it's the brand that suffers.

I still remember the old days clearly. When I was younger, our accountant would sit for hours with a calculator, manually crunching numbers for each employee. Come salary day, there'd be a queue of staff with complaints about hours missed or miscounted incentives. Then came desktop software—things improved. But today, AI can completely revolutionize the way we manage payroll and incentives in salons.

**Here's how AI is simplifying and optimizing salary calculations:**

### 1. Automated Salary + Incentive Calculations

AI can manage complex salary structures without errors:

- Fixed basic salary.
- Service-based incentives (e.g., ₹50 per facial, ₹100 per haircut beyond target).
- Retail product commissions (e.g., 10% on every product sold).

The system automatically pulls this data from your POS or appointment software, ensuring each stylist or therapist is paid accurately—based on real performance.

### 2. Performance-Based Analysis

AI doesn't just calculate—it also analyses:

- Number of clients handled.
- Type of services delivered (premium vs. basic).
- Client feedback scores.
- Retail sales volume.

It can then:

- Rank top performers.

- Suggest bonuses.
- Flag underperformance for coaching or follow-up.

### 3. Incentive Forecasting

AI can even predict incentives for motivation:

"If this stylist maintains current performance, she'll earn ₹5,000 in bonuses this month."

This kind of insight boosts morale and drives productivity.

### 4. Error-Free Payroll = Happy Staff

- AI eliminates human errors in calculation.
- Ensures fairness, transparency, and on-time salaries.
- Builds trust and keeps team spirits high.

### 5. Customizable Rules = Full Control

You can program your exact incentive rules into the system.

For example:

- ₹100 per service beyond 20 in a week
- 15% retail commission if sales cross ₹10,000/month

Once set, the software takes care of the rest. No manual adjustments would be needed.

### 6. Leave & Attendance Integration

AI can link with biometric or app-based attendance systems to:

- Auto-deduct late marks or absences.
- Track half-days or missed shifts This keeps both sides accountable and reduces salary disputes.

### 7. Reports & Dashboards in One Click

With AI tools, you can generate:

- Salary slips.

- Incentive breakdowns.
- Monthly payout summaries.

All instantly available to HR and the management for review or approval.

AI has turned what used to be a stressful, time-consuming monthly task into a smooth, accurate, and staff-friendly process. When your team sees their efforts translating into rewards—without delay or dispute—they'll stay longer, work better, and make your clients happier.

# CHAPTER 8

# MARKETING MOVES THAT MATTER: SMART MARKETING

## Know your Target Audience

It is very important to know who is your right target audience. We all have limited budgets to advertise. Within this budget, we need to showcase that we are the most suitable choice. Once we are clear about whom to target, the process becomes easier and filtered. For example, if your salon is targeting bridal makeups, then the offers, pictures, designs of advertising - all should reflect the charisma of marriage and importance of makeup. On the other hand if you are targeting young professionals, you may choose to offer express services and trendy styles.

**Knowing your audience helps you decide:**

- Where to advertise (Instagram for younger crowds, Facebook or local papers for older ones)
- What promotions to offer (student discounts, loyalty rewards, luxury

packages)

• How to speak their language (formal vs. casual tone, trendy vs. classic imagery)

## 1. Geographical locations can be marked:

We should evaluate and understand which all locations can be tapped. This implies not only an understanding of the state, district etc, but also location specifics like near offices, clubs, eating joints and many more such details.

For example if you are planning to launch a new hair colour in town, then capture the best of colleges, their canteens, gate side shops, and other popular joints. Posters can be made and placed there with attractive photographs of young girls and boys with the colour showcasing how confident they look after the use of the product. If you've noticed, in this example I have used all the points I had brought out in the para above. Advertise on the social media, by marking the geographical location, gender specific, age specific. This will help in reaching the right audience in the minimum budget.

## 2. Understand the competition:

One thing we all need to be honest about, is knowing that even if we think our idea is unique, we will still have competition around. The best way to shine brighter is to know your audience well, their needs and what the market is providing them at the moment. Then plan and create a pitch showing how what are you offering is different from others. Know your USPs and make them as the main pitch. This will directly resonate with the target audience and increase footfalls.

## 3. Train and Educate your Team

A salon is a part of the service industry which primarily runs on the skill and behaviour of the staff. So make sure you educate and train your staff in both these aspects. If the audience is being targeted for complicated services like skin treatments or advance hair colour, then you can hire and train staff in polished service skills and perhaps more advanced techniques. Only then will you be able to meet the expectations which the advertising claims.

### 4. Demographic Segmentation:

Demographic segmentation involves dividing the market based on demographic factors such as age, gender, income, education, and occupation. This type of segmentation helps businesses target specific groups of consumers based on easily measurable characteristics.

### 5. Story Sells

Storytelling allows salons to connect with customers on a deeper level by sharing relatable narratives. For example, a salon can tell the story of how their founder overcame personal beauty challenges and used that experience to create effective beauty solutions. One can even share the testimonial of their client, for a particular product that has helped them in maintaining healthy skin or hair while travelling daily to college or to office. However, ensure the story is real that is going on Reel.

### 6. Emotional Appeal:

This technique aims to evoke emotions and connect with customers on a personal level. Salons can share stories that focus on the emotional benefits of their products or services. For instance, a salon can narrate a story about a customer who regained her self-confidence through a transformative makeover, highlighting the emotional impact of their services.

### 7. Hero's Journey:

This technique follows the narrative structure of a hero's journey, where the protagonist faces challenges, undergoes transformation, and emerges victorious. Salons can use this technique to showcase the journey of their customers, or that of the owner emphasizing their beauty transformations and newfound confidence after experiencing their services.Women Empowerment, Men are Important, Earth is precious; Recycle Packaging, weight loss journeys are few of the famous ones.

### 8. Pricing Strategy

Last but not the least, the cost of the service will be the conversion and loyalty factor for any salon. Make sure your pricing aligns with what your target audience is willing to pay. The tried and tested formula is:

- Budget-friendly for students or lower-income neighbourhoods

- Premium pricing for luxury clientele
- Competitive packages for bridal and pre bridal services

Thus, it is important to know your target audience as it helps you make smart, focused decisions that attract and retain the right customers, increase satisfaction, and drive profitability. Without this clarity, your efforts can be scattered and less effective.

## Analyse the market every month:

Prevailing Trends change every now and then. You should always keep your eyes & ears open every month for small shifts in trends. Know the customer requests and make sure you track the trends popping up. You can get to know the latest launches and trends, by following social media, newspapers, beauty magazines and even TV shows.

I remember once, I looked completely blank when the client came and asked to replicate the look of the lead actress in the a very popular TV serial for her makeup. I had no clue as I had never seen that serial and had to google for reference and the reconfirm it to the client. Indeed, now days even a famous wedding happening, like that of big industrialist or of a Bollywood actress will bring about changes in the way of dressing the hair, accessories as well has make up. It may shift from glossy to absolute nude overnight. Thus, it is very important to stay updated and train yourself and your team accordingly.

### 1. Customers love to discover what's new

I have seen customers asking every time, "what's new?". They love to try the latest in the market. Trends change fast in beauty and wellness and you will have a Client suddenly wanting services like microblading, hair Botox, cryotherapy extra. Remember if you wait too long, they'll go to a competitor who already offers the service. Thereafter, getting the client back will be a difficult task.

### 2. Influential marketing

When any new brand, treatment, and tool drops in the market, everyone loves to try it and flaunt it on social media. Indeed, in case you are one of the first to launch a service, you could even invite some influencers and make them try your new launches. This is also a great content for social media. People will soon associate that your salon is the one who is always ahead in launching something new. Thus, you will be the new Trend Setter and talk of town.

### 3. Staff is always motivated

When you bring in new services, you create excitement and new learning for your team. The staff gets motivated and the retention is higher. It also gives them a chance to upsell and earn more, which boosts morale and performance. They love to learn the new technique and flaunt in front of client that there is something which the client can get only with them. They get a reason to do better sales and fulfil their monthly targets, and in the process, the salon sales will automatically increase.

### 4. You may charge premium

As the service is available only with you, you may charge a premium pricing for the same. Having the first mover advantage changes the game and makes you a pioneer of the art. This not only brings in more money and clientele, but also increases the chances of client being loyal to you, as she knows you will bring something good and advanced every time.

### 5. Boosts Online Booking & Website Traffic

When you are posting everything and taking regular google reviews of the clients, you will start ranking high, more people will click your website, check your Instagram, and hit "Book Now." You will have more booking and this will become a full circle.

*More views → More interest → More bookings*

## Marketing Tips & Tricks for a Salon

It is important for any salon to use few tips and tricks to score more clients with and without regular marketing. You just need to follow few rules and see that the brand value increases every day. The only key is to keep doing it, and never stop.

### 1. Keep the tone constant

From the logo to the colour scheme, and tone across all materials, keep it constant and aligned with each other. The brand should represent a clear message of being trendy, youth oriented or luxurious. This message should be clear and reflect in every form in which you advertise. Make sure the logo is clear and understandable. The advertisements should carry the same theme and the colour combinations too. This reflects the thought process and helps in building the brand value over a period of time.

### 2. Transformation stories

Post before & after transformations, client testimonials, and time-lapse videos on social media. This will attract more clients as it is very relatable. Each client gets the confidence that if you can transform a girl next door so beautifully, then she is opting for the right choice. Make sure you use trendy music and the latest transformations while making the reel. You never know what suddenly catches the market and makes the reel viral overnight. Study AI and make use of the algorithms of hashtags, location marking, etc to reach nearby clients.

### 3. Build a strong Google Business Profile

This is the basic necessity nowadays. Claim your Google listing with your correct location, hours, and photos. Make sure you collect and respond to Google Reviews regularly. This helps you appear in local search results, like "best salon near me." Positive reviews read by clients on Google create a good impact and make the decision to choose you as the next choice faster.

### 4. Opt for Referral Incentives

There is no publicity bigger than word of mouth publicity. Give both the referrer and the new customer a discount or free service. The client should be encouraged to bring a friend, and then earn rewards like 50 % off on her service for that day, while the friend too receives 25% off. You will see how the word spreads like fire and the clients multiply geometrically.

### 5. Run Limited-Time Offers

The best way to create a buzz in the market is by creating an urgency with short time offers. The client should feel it is a now or never deal. She should feel she should take the offer before it ends. The point to also consider is that do not extend the offer, otherwise the next time you run anything with ae timeline attached to it, the client might not understand the criticality of time and would remain casual to the offer. This might hamper the scheme rather than making it a success.

### 6. Market 360 degrees

When you plan any marketing, consider every possible place of advertisement. Be it social media, website banner, offline media like hoardings, cinema halls, TV, radio, print advertisements like pamphlets, leaflets, newspaper, magazines. Do what you can afford to, but choose multiple media. The client should see the same message on the street, which she saw on TV, or heard on radio while driving. Consider the technique of readvertising, something like , she has seen the add once on the internet, she sees the same add on other social media platforms too. All of them should carry the same message, tone, colour, actors etc. It should give a perfect recall value, indirectly forcing the client to go in for the service or the product, feeling that in case she does not, she will be left out. This will be like setting a trend in the market and will give better revenue.

### 7. Stronger local tie-ups

While you are trying to catch the attention of new clients by taking big steps as explained above, it is also important to do local grassroot level tie-ups. Cross-promote with nearby cafes, boutiques, or gyms. Put posters in their restrooms or billing counters and offer them the same facility in your salon. If they agree, keep a stack of discount card with their logo on it, and offer them small awards like a percentage in the billing, or a beauty service free, once the client comes in with the card and reference. This cross promotion serves as word of mouth publicity and increases the footfall without spending much.

## 8. Run Contests or Giveaways

Everyone likes to hear the tips and tricks for looking beautiful. Create content which attracts more and more audience in social media. Then add a contest with it, with giveaways being the product or a discount vouchers of your salon. When people win the salon voucher, they will surely walk in, as they value it more, since it is what they have won. The value is more than just a gift and thus the footfall is much more.

# CHAPTER 9

# THINKING BIGGER? LET'S TALK FRANCHISING

Once you plan to open a salon, you should have a clear vision to eventually franchise into multiple centres. It might seem unrealistic to some in the early stages, but if your salon is thriving and becoming a recognizable brand, franchising can be a powerful way to grow the Brand without taking on all the operational stress yourself.

Franchising your salon is like replicating your success. If your business model is stable and profitable, it's time to allow others to run with it under your brand name, while you stay focused on leading the vision. Offering your business model as a franchise can be a more strategic and financially sound option than opening company-owned outlets.

Here are **the types of franchising models in the salon industry**, explained in simple English:

### 1. FOFO – Franchise Owned, Franchise Operated

In this model, the franchisee invests their own money and also runs the salon operations.

The brand provides the name, training, and sometimes marketing support, but daily operations are handled by the franchisee.

**Ideal for:** Hands-on entrepreneurs who want full control.

**Examples:**

- Hiring and managing staff
- Handling daily collections
- Meeting monthly sales targets

### 2. FOCO – Franchise Owned, Company Operated

The franchisee invests, but the brand/company manages and runs the salon.

This is suitable for investors who want returns but don't want to be involved in daily operations.

**Ideal for**: Investors who want passive income from a reputed brand.

**Examples:**

- The brand hires and manages staff
- The company oversees operations and client handling
- Franchisee receives a share of profits or fixed returns

### 3. COCO – Company Owned, Company Operated

The salon is fully owned and operated by the company.

There is no franchisee involvement. These are direct company branches, often in flagship or strategic locations.

**Ideal for:** High-investment company-owned locations, pilot branches, or brand-controlled zones.

### 4. Hybrid Models

Some brands offer customized models, combining FOFO and FOCO — for example, franchisee handles investment and partial operations while the brand supports certain functions like training, audit, or software management.

## Why a Salon Should Franchise

### 1. Expand Without Your Own Investment

Franchising allows for quicker expansion without requiring your own capital. Opening multiple locations citywide, statewide, nationally, or even globally, demands significant investment. With franchising, your franchisees handle the costs of rent, staffing, and setup — reducing your financial risk.

It's crucial to select franchisees who not only believe in you and the brand but also have surplus capital. I recall my franchise marketing head bringing candidates who had just enough to open a salon, with no financial buffer. I used to turn them down — a decision that puzzled some colleagues. But I was clear: beyond the investment in franchise fees and setup, a franchisee must have funds to cover at least three months of operational costs with zero sales. When this condition is met, the franchise is far less likely to fail. In India, many salons close within six months due to cash flow issues. Unfortunately, when a franchise closes, the brand—not the individual franchisee—suffers reputational damage. So, always ensure prospective partners are financially equipped for at least three months of operations post-launch.

### 2. A New Revenue Stream Gets Created

Franchising generates various revenue streams:

- Initial franchise fees and ongoing royalties (either a percentage of sales or fixed cost).
- Increased demand for in-house manufactured products, boosting factory operations (as it did for my father's factory who was supplying for our 65 franchise branches).
- Monthly royalties that sustain the operational support team.
- Additional training sessions beyond standard packages.
- Examination fees from students enrolled at franchise centres.
- Profits from bulk-supplied, non-manufactured products stored in warehouses and distributed to franchises.

There are multiple directions to earn profit—you can adopt some or all of these based on your business model.

### 3. Strengthen Brand Presence

In business, quantity often supports market dominance. Imagine your salon having branches across the state, then the country, and eventually overseas. When I worked with Groom India, which operated over 800 salons, the pride and energy in the team were tangible. Now imagine your brand reaching such scale. Imagine your salon name in 800 outlets, what a smile and pride it is. That sense of credibility builds trust, draws in clients more easily, and cements your brand's place in the industry.

### 4. Choose Franchisees, Not Just Investors

Franchisees are more invested in the success of the salon than passive investors. They put in their own money and effort, ensuring higher standards in hygiene, service quality, and customer experience. They are more likely to follow Standard Operating Procedures (SOPs) and value training and brand guidelines. That effort has to be there, and not just money.

### 5. The Vision Expands

As you prepare to manage multiple centres, with recurring revenues, you'll naturally begin structuring a team with defined roles and responsibilities. Day-to-day fire-fighting gets delegated, allowing you to focus on branding, product innovation, marketing, and training. This shift builds your authority and opens new opportunities for partnerships, media coverage, and new verticals.

### 6. Launch Your Own Product Line

With a strong network of branches, launching your own line of branded products becomes a natural next step. This could be for in-house use or for retail. You can either set up your own manufacturing unit or partner with white-label factories that help develop products under your brand name. These partnerships cover everything from formulation to packaging, offering a scalable revenue model while enhancing brand uniqueness. Thus the brand becomes stronger in the market as now it promises equal role in retail as well as in the service.

## Summary Table

| Franchising | Company-Owned |
|---|---|
| Low capital requirement | High capital requirement |
| Rapid expansion possible | Slower, controlled growth |
| Franchisees highly motivated | Managers may lack ownership drive |
| Local knowledge & autonomy | Centralized control needed |
| Earn via fees & royalties | Earn through direct profits |
| Less operational burden | Full operational responsibility |

## Make the Franchise Plan Viable and Competitive

### Franchise Plan: A Profitable and Scalable Opportunity

You Have Created This Baby This salon brand is not just a business to you; it's your passion, your creation, and your pride. But in order to expand it successfully, it's essential to convey that same passion with a strong, convincing and practical business plan. Here's how you turn that love into a compelling case for franchising:

### 1. Financial Viability: A Sound Investment

Franchisees are putting their hard-earned money into your brand. They need more than emotional appeal—they need numbers. That's why your plan must show clear financial promise:

- **Setup Costs:** Clearly outline a reasonable, tier-based investment model. (e.g., Rs. 15-25 lakhs depending on location size and city tier).
- **Monthly Revenue Projection:** Provide data-backed estimates (e.g., Rs. 3-5 lakhs/month for Tier 1 cities).
- **Breakeven Timeline:** Design a model where breakeven is achievable within 12-18 months.
- **ROI:** Promise and prove an ROI within 2-3 years with market-backed proof.

With solid, well-researched financials, trust will follow.

### 2. Competitive Pricing: Win in a Crowded Market

Franchisees will compare your offer against others in the industry. They will be attending fairs like "Franchise India", your numbers and vision should speak louder than the competitors.

**Be ready with an offer that balances competitiveness and value:**

- **Initial Investment vs. Competitors:** Lower overhead with high brand value.
- **Franchise Fees & Royalty:** A fair and competitive percentage (e.g., 5-8% royalty).
- **High ROI with Controlled Costs:** Showcase how operational efficiency can boost profits.

### 3. Strong Support System: More Than Just a Brand

Franchisees choose you for your experience. Support is what turns a salon owner into a successful brand ambassador:

- **Staff Hiring & Training:** Standardized onboarding and regular refresher training modules.
- **Marketing Support:** National campaigns, social media content calendar, influencer collaborations.
- **Discounted Product Supply:** Tied-up vendors and exclusive pricing and discounts.
- **Salon Software & CRM:** Tech-enabled customer management and appointment systems.
- **Design & Location Help:** From space planning to aesthetics for each size and shape of the location.
- **Ongoing Digital Support:** Website listings, Google Maps setup, booking integrations.

The stronger your support, the lower their risk, and thus the option for selecting your brand will become stronger.

### 4. No Boundary Plan: Scale Without Limits

Franchisees could be from Mumbai or Meerut—your model must adapt:

- **Tier-Based Customization:** Packages adjusted for Tier 1, 2, and even 3 cities.
- **Cultural Adaptability:** Menu customization while keeping brand essence intact.
- **Global Scalability:** With minor adjustments, your salon can fit international markets too.

This flexibility makes your brand truly scalable.

### 5. Less Complication = Better Results

Franchisees appreciate transparency. No jargon. No ambiguity.

Clearly explain:

- **Total Investment and monthly expenses**
- **What They Get:** Setup kit, branding material, pre-opening training.

- **Ongoing Fees:** Royalty, software subscription (if any).
- **Your Deliverables:** What you provide, when, and how.

Clarity builds confidence.

### 6. Offer Unique Selling Points (USPs)

In a saturated salon industry, your USP is the deal-maker. What makes your brand the one to invest in? When I sold major franchise of Bharti Taneja's Alps and even got an award for opening 40 centres over the span of a year my pitch was the USP. That time it was the only brand whose owner was reachable herself. She was the brand name, as big as any celebrity in the beauty world, but also completely grounded and reachable, once the need arose. So, a common person would feel inspired and yet connected.

**Other examples:**

- **Founder Access:** A personal connect with the brand founder.
- **Signature Services:** Only-salon-in-region to offer X facial or Y hair ritual.
- **Eco-Friendly Practices:** Sustainable products, zero-plastic packaging.
- **High Hygiene Standards:** Hospital-grade sterilization protocols.
- **Loyalty Programs:** Digital rewards system for customers.

Your USP must be real, relatable, and revenue-driving. It's not just a point of difference—it's a reason to choose you.

A franchise plan is not just a document—it's your promise. The clearer, more profitable, and professional it looks, the more confident a franchisee will be in joining your journey.

This isn't just business expansion. It's a brand family growing with shared values, mutual goals, and collective success.

## Draft the Legal Papers Well and Abide by Them

Carefully Prepare the Franchise Agreement & Abide by The Clauses:

When you are planning to expand the brand, a Legal Advisor is the person who should be your best friend. I learned this after spending a week preparing the papers for my own brand when expansion was on my mind. The lawyer I worked with, made me understand how important it is to know everything from your rights to your duties, and we applied the these principles in drafting the franchise papers.

A franchise agreement isn't just paperwork — it's the foundation of a business partnership. Hiring a legal firm isn't an expense — it's an investment in protection, professionalism, and peace of mind.

You must keep these points in mind when you are getting the documents drafted:

**1. Brand Protection**

o The agreement should protect your brand name, logo, and registered names or slogans.

o Specific details such as logo colour, font, and proper usage should be included to prevent misuse by the franchisee.

**2. Roles and Responsibilities**

o Clearly define what the franchisor provides (training, marketing, product supply, etc.).

o Clearly define what the franchisee must handle (staffing, rent, daily operations, local marketing, etc.).

o This avoids confusion, assumptions, and future disputes.

**3. Essential Clauses**

o Franchise fees

o Royalty structure (monthly percentage or fixed)

o Payment timelines

o Late payment penalties

o Terms of renewal or non-renewal

- o Exit strategy for either party
- o Exclusive territory rights for franchisee, if applicable
- o Consequences and next steps if any of the above terms are not fulfilled

**4. Breach, Termination & Dispute Resolution**

- o Define what qualifies as a breach of agreement
- o Specify when and how either party can terminate the contract
- o Detail where and how disputes will be resolved (arbitration or court)

A well-drafted franchise agreement is critical to long-term success and smooth operations. It's not just a formality; it's the blueprint of your business relationship.

## Regular Observation of Franchise Reports

### Regular Monitoring and Reporting

o Many franchisors make the mistake of only checking reports during the initial days and then becoming relax as expansion grows. This unprofessional approach often results in declining standards.

o Trust is important, but regular audits and performance checks are essential.

### Why Regular Monitoring is Crucial:

**o Sales and Profit Reports:**

- Identify top-performing and underperforming services.
- Adapt the steps taken by top performing salons to others so that their sales increases too.
- Take corrective actions early to prevent losses.

**o Staff Performance Reports:**

- Monitor employee attendance, client feedback, and service quality.
- If any of the above has any discrimpencies, then solve it in the initial step, before it gets too late and you need to face the consequences.
- Staff directly impact customer satisfaction and profit margins.

**o Client Feedback:**

- Track complaints, reviews, and feedback regularly.
- Identify recurring issues (e.g., poor service, wait times, hygiene concerns).
- Discuss with the owner as well as with the staff.
- Address grievances quickly to prevent negative online reviews.

**o Marketing Performance:**

- Assess which campaigns are driving salon traffic.
- Add and subtract the budget specifics.

  - Measure ROI from discounts, promotions, or paid ads.

- **Inventory Reports:**
  - Track overstocking or shortages of key products.
  - Monitor product expiry dates to avoid wastage.

- **Trend Analysis:**
  - Spot early warning signs like revenue drops or staff underperformance.
  - Take immediate corrective measures before issues scale up.
  - Add new trends and improve the sales in each field and centre.

Staying vigilant through consistent reporting not only strengthens the brand but also upholds the professional standards of the franchise. This habit ensures continued alignment with your short-term targets and long-term vision.

## Remember they are your partners and not your employees

This is something I want to really highlight. When we are searching for a franchise, we are in desperate need and want to sign every person we meet. Slowly, the brand becomes bigger and we become choosers in the selection process. This slow behavioural change affects how we treat our partners. We often forget to maintain the distinction between franchisees as partners or investors and employees. This distinction is key to a successful franchise relationship and sets the right tone for how both parties work together.

Its like marriage between the two companies. Thus it is very important to manage the relationship, and there are effective ways to do so:

### 1. Set Clear Expectations from the Start:

Clear expectations prevent misunderstandings, conflicts, and misaligned goals from the very beginning. Ensure the franchise agreement is clear on the responsibilities of both the franchisor and the franchisee. Before the agreement is signed, have an open conversation about expectations, goals, and objectives to ensure alignment. This establishes a clear line of duty and fosters mutual respect.

### 2. Provide Consistent Support and Training:

Offer comprehensive initial training on all aspects of running the salon franchise — from customer service to operations and marketing. Conduct regular check-ins, refresher courses, and continued training to ensure franchisees stay updated with new techniques, products, or services. This not only boosts franchisee morale but also leads to happier staff and consistent business inflow, aiding smooth royalty collection.

### 3. Create Open Communication Channels:

Often, we pay attention only to the "crying baby," while the quiet franchisee gets neglected. We assume no news is good news and minimize communication. It is essential to schedule monthly or quarterly meetings to review performance, discuss challenges, and celebrate successes. Whether through in-person meetings, video calls, or emails, regular communication maintains strong relationships. Two-way communication keeps both parties engaged and ensures timely resolution of issues.

### 4. Monitor Performance and Offer Constructive Guidance:

Don't just monitor, but also provide guidance for better sales and improvements. Show that you care and are not just an auditor. Require monthly sales and performance reports from franchisees. Use these to analyse trends, ensure operational standards, and identify improvement areas. Discuss findings with the franchisee, focusing on solutions and growth opportunities instead of mistakes.

### 5. Offer Marketing and Branding Support:

Provide marketing materials like posters, flyers, digital ads, and localized promotional content. Empower franchisees to customize marketing while maintaining brand standards. Organize joint campaigns or promotions that include franchisee participation. Share the results of national or regional marketing efforts.

### 6. Recognize and Reward Success:

Reward top-performing franchisees with bonuses, franchise fee discounts, or recognition at company events. Acknowledge their hard work, celebrate milestones, and visit them personally to build relationships. Recognition fosters loyalty and helps franchisees feel valued as partners. A happy franchisee base can lead to exponential business growth.

### 7. Ensure a Clear Exit or Transition Process:

Clearly outline the process for exiting or transferring a franchise well in advance. Include procedures for franchise sale, brand deactivation, rebranding, and agreement termination. Assist franchisees in preparing for transitions, whether selling, passing on the business, or closing it. Ensure this process is clear, respectful, and organized. A considerate exit process can ease tensions and preserve relationships, even in loss.

By treating franchisees as true partners and investing in their success, a franchise brand can build a strong, loyal, and high-performing network that grows sustainably over time.

# CHAPTER 10

# ARE YOU GROWING? LET'S MEASURE

Growth is a broad term that encompasses wealth accumulation, brand building, personal development, and psychological advancement. There are various methods to evaluate and adjust it regularly. I recall that when I first joined my business, one of our salons was underperforming in terms of sales. Despite our continued investment to improve it, we saw minimal returns. Taking a day off, I sat down with my financial advisor and, by the end of the day, we concluded that the salon needed to be closed. It was not only eroding the profits of our other locations but had also become an emotional burden. Though it was a difficult decision, sometimes tough choices are necessary. I sold it for a minimal amount. I vividly remember how we had selected every tile and mirror with care and precision. Yet, when the audit reveals consistent losses with no signs of recovery, it's time to move on.

Yes, analysis might uncover losses, but it also helps identify weak spots and highlights the progress made compared to previous periods. Addressing issues head-on is crucial. Don't ignore the problems; take proactive steps to resolve them. This approach will drive you toward not just more sales, but significantly increased profits.

## Use Audit to Catch Leakages Monthly

Conducting regular audits is essential—and doing so monthly is even more critical. Monthly audits help in detecting and preventing recurring issues, ensuring that the same mistakes are not repeated. Identifying and fixing these leakages early will safeguard the health of your business and contribute to sustained growth.

It is important to audit, and equally important to audit monthly. This will avoid the repetition of leakages, if any, for the upcoming months:

### 1. Track Revenue

It is important to track sales for every service, deposited in every bank and collected as cash in the salon. Keep in the mind the sales form daily work, product sold, credit received if any and the bigger amount from the packages booked. If needed, use a point-of-sale (POS) system to streamline this process. Analyse every earning and put them in the right category. See from which service you are getting more, identify fast moving products, which scheme is doing well and even compare sales on weekdays vis-a-vis weekends.

### 2. Track Expenses

Categorize your expenses into daily and monthly expenses:

o **Rent:** monthly rent to the owner of the location plus the maintenance rent to the mall or shopping area, if any, for the utilities you use. If the property is yours, just keep in mind the house tax.

o **Product costs:** Amount spent in purchasing products for use like shampoos, conditioners, hair colour, nail polish, etc. Also keep a track of the retail products in the store.

o **Staff wages:** Salaries plus overtime along with the commission-based pay for the manager and other staff.

o **Supplies:** Towels, aprons, cleaning products, etc.

o **Marketing:** Advertising costs, social media promotions, or loyalty programs.

o **Equipment maintenance:** Repair or replacement of equipment like hairdryers, chairs, etc.

o **Area maintenance:** The maintenance of the store like paint, AC service, RO service extra.

o **Insurances and Warranties:** Keep a record where you are renewing nsurances or warranties for equipment, fire accidents etc.

o **Free services:** You may have to give few services free to a friend, or a relative once in a month or so. Keep this also on record when you are counting the expenses. This is equally important as I could see loads of our relatives hopping in the salon saying " I need little bit of makeup, hair style and a simple facial, nothing much." And when I used to tell them to sign a gift voucher of Rs. 12,000 for the free services, they and even I used to realize how much I have invested on them. So, simply keep a record.

o **Festive expenses:** there are few expenses which happen during festivals like Holi and Deepawali, like the Kinnars and others who collect money from each shop in the locality. The extra boxes of sweets and gifts for staff s well as the utility workers etc. keep a record of these as the additional surprise, but sure shot, expense.

### 3. Calculate Gross Profit

Gross Profit = **Total Revenue – Cost of Products Consumed (COPC)**

- **COPC** includes the cost of products used directly for services (massage cream, hair colour, pedicure shampoo, etc.).
- If the gross profit is less then there are either of the two problems:

o The rate of the service is less.

o The product consumed is more expensive

**For example:** You suggested a facial to the client. The cost of the facial kit is Rs 250, plus the cotton, the disposable gown and the towels are for Rs. 50. There is an offer ongoing in the salon, which says "buy one and get one free". If you are charging the client Rs 300 for the facial you are making a huge mistake. In the gross profit. Next will also be the count of the service, salary, rent, electricity and extra machines used. This is a perfect example of miscalculation .

- A high gross profit margin indicates your services and products are priced correctly and that you are managing direct costs efficiently.

### 4. Calculate Operating Profit

Operating Profit = **Gross Profit – Operating Expenses**

- Operating expenses are your fixed and variable overhead costs, including rent, utilities, staff wages, and marketing. This is the "real" profit or loss from your salon operations.

• If the operating profit is less then there are either of the following problems:

o Rent of the place is high.

o The staff kept are more in numbers or they have higher salaries than the work they are getting every day.

o Your marketing expenses are eating all the profits.

### 5. Track Labor Costs

Labor costs should be a major area of focus, as they can heavily impact profitability:

• Calculate **Labor Cost Percentage:** (Labor Costs ÷ Revenue) x 100.

• A typical target is around 40%–50% of total revenue, but this can vary, based on the salon's size, location, and business model.

### 6. Net Profit or Loss

Net Profit (or Loss) = **Operating Profit – Taxes and other expenses.**

• Once all operating expenses and taxes are accounted for, the result will show whether your salon made a profit or suffered a loss for the month.

• Remember to count yourself as an employee and pay salary to yourself too. You know your market cost, so don't forget to reward yourself too.

### 7. Cash Flow Analysis

• **Cash Inflow:** Monitor cash entering the business (service sales, retail products, etc.).

• **Cash Outflow:** Track all cash spent (rent, payroll, inventory purchases, utilities, etc.).

• Ensure there is enough cash flow to cover expenses; negative cash flow over time can indicate potential problems.

### 8. Review Key Performance Indicators (KPIs)

Track KPIs regularly to understand your salon's performance:

- **Client Retention Rate:** The percentage of clients who return for repeat services. You may manage this in the software, or in the ledger by giving a full page to the individual client and noting down every time she has used the services in the salon.

- **Average Revenue Per Client:** This is the total revenue divided by the number of clients served. This is very important as you might be serving many clients, but the revenue would be lesser. This can be due to the less rates of the services or client opting for smaller services or asking for more discounts at the counter.

- **Average Service Price:** Average price per service, which helps in pricing adjustments. Do note the average bill value per client. Analysis of this will reveal a lot about the rates and the client's trust on the brand. This can be edited by counselling the client and marketing the higher rate services in an attractive manner.

- **Retail Sales per Client:** This is the average amount spent by clients on retail products. An analysis of this will also reveal two things. First, which is the highest selling product and brand. Second, are the employees making sure to sell retail products on a regular basis or do they need further training for the same.

### 9. Profitability Ratios

Use these ratios to evaluate how efficiently the salon is operating:

- **Gross Margin Ratio:** (Gross Profit ÷ Revenue) x 100. This will show the profitability from core operations.

- **Net Profit Margin:** (Net Profit ÷ Revenue) x 100. This is the final profitability after all expenses.

### 10. Compare Monthly Trends

- **Seasonal Fluctuations:** Consider if revenue or expenses fluctuate due to seasonality (e.g., holidays, weather, wedding season).

- **Year-Over-Year Comparison:** Compare monthly results with the same month in the previous year to track growth or identify trends. While doing these calculations, keep in mind to cater for annual inflation also.

### 11. Look for Red Flags

- **Excessive overhead costs:** If fixed costs are growing faster than revenue, it could indicate inefficiencies or overspending.

- **Declining revenue:** If sales are consistently going down, look into customer satisfaction, competition, or potential market changes.

**I would also add in bold:**

*Don't ignore the red flags at all.*

*Make sure you analyse the correct problem and act on it immediately.*

## 12. Prepare Financial Statements

Prepare a monthly income statement (profit and loss statement) and balance sheet to summarize:

- **Income Statement:** Shows revenues, expenses, and profits over the month.

- **Balance Sheet:** Details the salon's assets, liabilities, and equity, which can help assess its overall financial health.

## 13. Adjustments and Improvements

Have you ever calculated all of the above points when you thought the centre is doing well and you are happy with the sales? Many a times, when the sale of the day is good, we feel that the salon is profitable and vice versa. We actually do not calculate the above points as a complete cycle. Based on the audit, adjust pricing, reduce unnecessary expenses, or streamline operations to improve profitability in the next month.

By following the above steps, you can get a clear picture of whether your salon is making a profit or running at a loss each month. Regular audits will also help you in identifying areas for improvement and keep your salon's finances on track.

## Invest in a Financial Advisor

Like I emphasised earlier on investing in a good legal person for the company, it is equally important to have a good financial advisor for the same reason. Appointing a financial advisor for your salon can be highly beneficial in guiding you towards better sales and profitability. While managing the finances of a salon might seem manageable at first, the complexities of balancing cash flow, client acquisition, and overall profitability can quickly add up and coupled with managing other things, it will become unmanageable. A financial advisor brings the expertise needed to optimize your salon's financial performance, allowing you to focus on the core aspects of running your business—serving clients and delivering quality services. The guidance of the financial advisor can be the difference between steady growth and financial struggles.

Here are several key reasons why having a Financial Advisor important:

- **Strategic Planning:** A financial advisor can help you create a financial plan tailored to your salon's unique needs, including budgeting, forecasting, and managing cash flow. This strategy ensures that you are focusing on the right areas to maximize profits and minimize costs.

- **Investment Decisions:** If you're looking to invest in new services or products or to expand your salon, open additional locations; a financial advisor can guide you in making informed decisions, ensuring you're not overspending or taking unnecessary financial risks.

- **Cash Flow Management:** With wedding seasons and weather fluctuations, salon businesses often experience fluctuations in cash flow, especially with seasonality or client volume variations. A financial advisor helps you track and optimize cash flow so you can manage day-to-day operations smoothly, cover expenses, and avoid liquidity problems.

- **Expense Management:** Many a times we do not come to know where we are overspending. By analysing your expenses, a financial advisor can identify these areas and suggest cost-cutting measures without sacrificing quality.

- **Revenue Growth:** Financial advisors can help identify opportunities for increasing revenue, such as adjusting service pricing, introducing new services, or improving client retention strategies. They can also recommend more effective ways of marketing and upselling to boost sales.

- **Margin Analysis:** A financial advisor can assess your gross profit margin (services vs. products) and recommend pricing or operational changes that could improve profitability. They may also provide insights into cost-of-goods-sold (COGS) or used in service, and how you can lower them to boost profits.

- **Tax Efficiency:** A financial advisor can guide you on tax-saving strategies, including business deductions, tax credits, and planning for quarterly or annual taxes. Their expertise ensures you're not overpaying in taxes and taking advantage of any available tax benefits specific to small businesses, in addition to filling the income tax returns regularly.

- **Compliance:** A financial advisor will ensure your salon is compliant with all tax laws, accounting standards, and industry regulations, preventing potential fines or audits.

- **Regular Financial Monitoring:** A financial advisor can prepare monthly, quarterly, and yearly financial statements (P&L, balance sheets, and cash flow) that offer valuable insights into your salon's financial health. This allows you to make more informed decisions - based on data, not guesswork.

- **KPI Tracking:** A financial advisor will help you track key performance indicators (KPIs) like client retention, average revenue per client, and labour costs, ensuring you stay on target for your profit goals.

- **Budget Creation:** A financial advisor helps you set realistic budgets for expenses like marketing, payroll, inventory, and capital investments. They will also assist in creating realistic revenue forecasts based on historical data, helping you plan for slow seasons or periods of expansion.

- **Cost Reduction:** Finance experts can audit your current expenses to find opportunities for cost savings without compromising the customer experience. For example, they might suggest switching suppliers, reducing waste, or renegotiating contracts with vendors.

- **Inventory Management:** Financial advisors can analyse your salon's inventory usage and product sales to identify slow-moving products or excess stock, optimizing inventory levels and reducing waste.

- **Business Growth Strategy:** A financial advisor can help map out the financial implications of expanding your salon, taking on new debt, or increasing your workforce. Their guidance ensures you're making the right financial moves for long-term sustainability and growth.

- **Loans and Financing:** If you need capital for expansion, renovation, or equipment upgrades, a financial advisor can help you explore the best financing options—whether through business loans, lines of credit, or investor funding—ensuring you make the right choice without over-leveraging.

- **Personalized Advice:** A financial advisor can offer personalized recommendations based on the salon's specific challenges, goals, and market conditions, providing tailored advice that a one-size-fits-all approach might miss.

## Pay Regular Taxes

We might crib every time we need to pay taxes, or calculate and recalculate the changes whenever the budget is announced. But, paying regular taxes when running a salon in India comes with several important benefits. Here are the key advantages:

### 1. Legal Compliance and Avoidance of Penalties

- **Avoid Legal Issues:** Paying your taxes regularly ensures that your salon complies with Indian tax laws, reducing the risk of legal trouble. Non-payment or under-reporting of taxes can lead to penalties, fines, or even legal action by the authorities.

- **Avoid Penalties:** The Income Tax Department and other regulatory bodies impose fines and penalties for non-compliance, which can accumulate over time and severely impact your salon's profitability.

- **Tax Audits:** By paying taxes regularly and maintaining proper records, you reduce the likelihood of a tax audit, as the authorities will view you as a compliant business.

### 2. Eligibility for Business Loans and Financial Support

- **Improved Credit Worthiness:** Regular tax payments improve your salon's credit profile, making it easier to obtain loans or financial support from banks and financial institutions when needed. Lenders and investors often look at your tax compliance to assess the financial health and reliability of your business. Sibil score is the mirror of the growth of the salon.

- **Government Schemes:** By paying taxes on time, you become eligible for government schemes or incentives aimed at supporting small businesses, such as the MSME (Micro, Small, and Medium Enterprises) schemes, which often require proof of tax compliance. Indeed, they have schemes in which you can participate in various exhibitions with absolutely no cost and display the services and the products. All these need records of at least three years of your income tax returns.

### 3. Building a Strong Business Reputation

- **Trust with Clients and Partners:** Paying taxes regularly enhances your business's credibility and reputation in the market. It shows that you are running a transparent and responsible operation, which can attract clients, suppliers, and partners who value compliance.

- **Increased Client Confidence:** Clients are more likely to trust a salon that adheres to the law, which could result in repeat business, referrals, and better customer loyalty.

### 4. Tax Benefits and Deductions

- **Business Expense Deductions:** Regular tax filings allow you to claim various business expenses as deductions, reducing your taxable income and ultimately lowering the amount of tax you owe. These can include expenses like employee salaries, rent, utility bills, product costs, marketing expenses, and more.

- **Depreciation Deductions:** You can claim depreciation on salon equipment and furniture, which will reduce your taxable income and, in turn, lower the taxes you need to pay.

- **GST Input Tax Credit:** If your salon is registered under GST (Goods and Services Tax), you can avail yourself of the input tax credit for the GST you pay on business-related purchases, which can be deducted from the GST you owe on your salon's sales.

### 5. Financial Planning and Growth

- **Better Financial Management:** Regular tax payments encourage better financial management and budgeting. Paying taxes forces you to keep detailed financial records, which can be a valuable tool for assessing your business's financial health and making informed decisions.

- **Improved Business Growth:** By staying compliant with tax laws, you build a solid financial foundation for your salon, making it easier to plan for growth, expansion, or investment in new equipment and services.

### 6. Avoiding Interest on Late Payments

- **Interest-Free:** By paying taxes on time, you avoid paying interest on late payments, which can accumulate and affect your profitability. The Income Tax Department levies interest under sections like 234A, 234B, and 234C if taxes are not paid on time.

- **Timely Filing Benefits:** When you pay taxes regularly and file returns on time, you avoid interest charges that can negatively impact your salon's financial situation.

### 7. Business Continuity and Licenses

- **Compliance for Licenses:** Many state and central government licenses or permits require proof of tax compliance. These may include health and safety licenses, trade licenses, and GST registration. Regular tax payment helps in maintaining these licenses, which are crucial for the continued operation of your salon.

- **Avoiding Business Shutdown:** Non-payment of taxes can result in the suspension of your business operations or confiscation of assets. Regular tax payments ensure smooth operations without interruption.

### 8. Support for Local Economy

- **Contributing to Public Services:** Paying taxes helps fund local infrastructure, health, education, and public services that indirectly benefit your salon. A well-developed infrastructure—such as roads, transportation, and utilities—can improve your salon's accessibility and attract more customers.

- **Strengthening the Economy:** Regular tax payment supports the broader economy, which in turn benefits all businesses, including salons, by contributing to a stable and growing economy.

### 9. Social Responsibility

- **Ethical Responsibility:** Paying taxes demonstrates your salon's commitment to social responsibility. It's an ethical practice that supports national development and contributes to society, which can foster goodwill within the community.

- **Boosts Reputation Among Employees:** Being a responsible taxpayer can also inspire trust and respect from your employees, who will feel more secure working for a business that is legally compliant and stable.

### 10. Planning for Future Growth

- **Retirement Plans and Succession:** Regular tax payments create a stable financial foundation that makes it easier to plan for the future of the business. Whether you plan to retire, sell the salon, or pass it on to a successor, having a clear and clean financial record is essential for any transition.

- **Risk Management:** Tax compliance helps you reduce the risk of sudden financial setbacks or surprises, enabling smoother transitions during business expansions, acquisitions, or other changes.

## Give yourself a salary

This is one of my favourite pieces of advice. I have seen salon owners, paying everyone and in the end investing the savings, but not rewarding themselves anything. After few months of work, they feel as if they are working for the staff and being an owner of the salon has not given them any monetary satisfaction. Giving yourself a salary as a business owner, especially when running a salon or any small business, is an important practice for both personal and business motivation. Here's why it can be so beneficial:

### 1. Ensures Financial Stability and Security

- **Personal Income:** By paying yourself a salary, you create a predictable income stream for your personal expenses, which ensures you can cover your living costs without relying on business profits that may fluctuate.

- **Separate Personal and Business Finances:** Paying yourself a fixed salary helps you keep your personal and business finances separate, which is important for both financial planning and tax purposes. This distinction makes it easier to track business performance and avoid mixing business funds with personal funds.

### 2. Professional Mindset

- **Treating Your Business Like a Business:** Paying yourself a salary establishes a professional attitude toward your business. It reinforces the mindset that the business is not just a hobby, but an entity that generates revenue and should function with proper financial discipline.

- **Structure and Accountability:** A salary provides structure to your financial habits. Just like paying employees regularly, giving yourself a salary ensures that you follow a consistent payroll schedule, fostering good financial practices and discipline.

### 3. Motivation and Commitment

- **Personal Motivation:** Having a salary motivates you to keep the business running profitably. It makes you more committed to ensuring that the business performs well and grows, knowing that you are dependent on it for your personal income. The pride of self-earned money has its own charm.

- **Reward for Hard Work:** As the owner, you often work long hours and face numerous challenges. A regular salary provides a tangible reward for your efforts and sacrifices, which can boost your morale and help avoid burnout. Imagine treating yourself with a short trip or just that perfect brunch in a five star property, which you had kept in your bucket list for a long time, makes you happy for days to come.

### 4. Encourages Better Business Practices

- **Cash Flow Awareness:** When you pay yourself a salary, you're forced to regularly assess the salon's cash flow to ensure you can afford it. This awareness helps you better manage the business's finances, avoid overspending, and make more informed decisions about pricing, costs, and investments. You will understand that you too have a limit on spending the money and rest is your savings. This way you won't end up overspending whatever you have earned.

- **Long-Term Planning:** By paying yourself a salary, you're also creating a framework for sustainable growth. A consistent income means that you're thinking about both short-term and long-term financial stability, rather than just relying on irregular profits or taking all the money out of the business.

### 5. Tax Benefits and Planning

- **Taxable Income:** Paying yourself a salary makes your income subject to regular tax deductions at source (TDS). This ensures you are compliant with tax laws, avoiding penalties or audits in the future.

- **Deductions for Business:** As a salaried individual within your own business, you may be able to deduct your salary as a business expense, reducing the overall taxable profit of the business. This can lead to potential tax savings.

### 6. Establishes Financial Discipline for Growth

- **Profit Allocation:** Paying yourself a fixed salary helps you allocate profits toward reinvestment in the business, such as upgrading equipment, marketing, or expanding services. It prevents you from spending all the profits on personal expenses, which can sometimes hurt the business's long-term growth.

- **Clear Business Goals:** Having a salary means you're separating what's personally yours and what's meant for the business. This gives you the ability to focus on business reinvestment and growth while ensuring your personal financial needs are met without compromising on the salon's development.

### 7. Fosters Professional Relationships

- **Employee Relations:** If you have staff, paying yourself a salary establishes fairness and shows that you value your own time and work. It helps maintain a professional dynamic with your employees, as they see that you're not just extracting all the business's profits but rather treating yourself as an equal employee. This is one of the ways in which I have always remained grounded in spite of being the owner of chain of salons.

- **Setting an Example:** Paying yourself a salary sets a positive example for employees. It shows that you value consistent work and effort, creating a healthy culture of respect for work-life balance and financial responsibility. You will surely notice how the staff values this.

### 8. Avoiding Burnout

- **Work-Life Balance:** Without a salary, it can be tempting to sacrifice personal time and wellbeing for the sake of the business, which can lead to burnout. A salary forces you to balance your time and resources, making it easier to take breaks, pay attention to your personal needs, and avoid working excessively without reward. Make sure you spend this in fulfilling your bucket list of travel or shopping. This will make the point exciting. I have seen many salons owner spending their salaries for better education of their kids, which is also a feeling of ultimate satisfaction. I always say "each one to its own", but do use this extra income in the manner it satisfies you.

- **Financial Cushion for Mental Peace:** Knowing that you have a regular income coming in provides peace of mind, allowing you to focus on growing the business rather than constantly worrying about whether the salon can generate enough profit to cover your living costs.

### 9. Psychological Value and Personal Satisfaction

- **Feelings of Achievement:** Paying yourself a regular salary gives you a tangible acknowledgment of your hard work. It reinforces the idea that your efforts are paying off and that your salon business is successful enough to support you. Imagine, if you were not running this outlet, you would have been working in some salon and getting a regular pay check in the end of the month. So, feel that reward of the hard work done every month.

- **Work Satisfaction:** It psychologically encourages you to treat your business with the seriousness and respect it deserves. A salary makes you feel more like a "business owner" and less like someone scrambling to make ends meet, thus improving overall satisfaction with your work.

### 10. Clear Succession and Exit Strategy

- **Valuing Your Business:** When you pay yourself a salary, it's easier to value your business when the time comes to sell it or transition to another phase of life. Potential buyers or investors will see the salary as an indicator of the business's profitability and structure.

- **Exit Planning:** If you ever plan to retire or hand over the business, a clear salary structure allows for smoother transition planning, making it easier to define your role and the business's operations in the future.

## Take corrective action without delaying

When you find a flaw or a loss in a financial audit, it's crucial to take immediate action. The sooner you address the issue, the better, and here's why:

### 1. Prevents Escalation of Problems

- **Mitigating Larger Losses:** Small financial issues, if left unaddressed, can quickly grow into much larger problems. For instance, unnoticed over-spending or under-pricing can lead to a significant cash flow crisis. The quicker you act, the more you can minimize potential losses and prevent the situation from becoming worse. On the other hand, if you keep on avoiding the problem, it might be too late to solve.

- **Prevent Accumulation of Interest or Penalties:** If the issue involves unpaid taxes or missed payments, addressing it quickly prevents you from incurring late fees, interest, or penalties, which can compound over time and severely damage the financial health of the business.

### 2. Improves Cash Flow Management

- **Maintaining Liquidity:** By identifying a flaw early, you can take corrective action to protect your salon's cash flow. Poor cash flow is one of the most common reasons why businesses fail. By reacting quickly, you can ensure the salon has enough liquidity to cover expenses and keep running smoothly.

- **Replenishing Reserves:** If the audit reveals that you're spending too much on supplies or wages, taking action promptly can help you control costs, thus improving your cash flow and profitability. If the need arises, you may have to reduce the staff or edit their wages for a particular time period. Sometimes the problem can be sorted by changing the product brands, or even selecting vendors who provide better deals.

### 3. Keeps the Business Compliant

- **Tax and Regulatory Compliance:** If the audit uncovers issues related to taxes, licenses, or other legal obligations, taking prompt action is essential for staying compliant. Non-compliance can lead to fines, penalties, or even legal action. Immediate corrective steps help avoid these risks.

- **Record Accuracy:** Financial audits are used to verify the accuracy of business records. If discrepancies are found, acting quickly ensures that your records are updated and correct, helping you maintain transparency with authorities and stakeholders.

### 4. Maintains Business Reputation

- **Trust and Credibility:** If customers or suppliers see that you're addressing financial issues promptly and efficiently, it builds trust and confidence in your business. Customers appreciate working with a business that is financially stable and reliable.

- **Employee Morale:** If employees notice financial discrepancies or losses but see that you're taking swift action to correct them, it reassures them that the business is on track and that they have job security. This helps maintain morale and keeps the team focused and motivated. Else, if they notice that you are unaware or do not take any action, even after noticing, they might feel that their job is at the risk as when the time of cost cutting will arise during an emergency, they will surely be the first ones to be affected.

### 5. Allows for Timely Adjustments

- **Pricing Adjustments:** If an audit reveals that your prices are too low or that the cost of goods sold is too high, taking action quickly allows you to make pricing adjustments or renegotiate supplier contracts. This can restore profitability and prevent further financial strain.

- **Cost-Cutting Measures:** If operational inefficiencies are found, you can take action immediately to cut unnecessary expenses. For example, if you're spending too much on utilities or waste, addressing it right away helps ensure you're using resources more efficiently. Opting for a different brand of products with the same quality but a better pricing can also be opted for.

### 6. Helps with Long-Term Planning

- **Informed Decisions:** Early action based on audit findings enables you to make informed decisions about the future. Whether it's adjusting your financial strategy, renegotiating vendor contracts, or improving customer acquisition, quick fixes can pave the way for more strategic long-term planning.

- **Budgeting for the Future:** If the audit reveals that certain costs are spiralling out of control, taking action allows you to adjust future budgets accordingly and plan for the next financial year without these issues looming over you.

### 7. Reduces Risk of Fraud or Theft

- **Identifying Fraud:** Sometimes financial audits uncover fraudulent activity or theft. Addressing these issues immediately by investigating, securing evidence, and involving legal authorities (if needed) is crucial to prevent further losses. Taking prompt action can minimize the impact and deter potential fraudsters. I remember my stock keeper and the receptionist becoming best of buddies and selling products without a bill. Once we traced out the problem, we had to get rid of both of them on the same day. This would have continued for months together if we had delayed the audit.

- **Internal Controls:** A timely response to financial issues can lead to strengthening of internal controls and financial processes to prevent future occurrences of fraud or mismanagement.

## 8. Enhances Decision-Making Ability

- **Real-Time Insights:** When you act on audit findings quickly, you have a clearer picture of your salon's financial situation in real time. This enables you to make better business decisions based on the most up-to-date and accurate information.

- **Faster Problem-Solving:** Addressing financial flaws quickly leads to more rapid problem-solving and adaptability. Whether you need to increase sales, cut costs, or adjust operations, quick action gives you the agility to navigate challenges effectively. Something as simple as reducing wastage of that extra colour taken for the client in a bowl and then thrown in the sink, as the amount was miscalculated, is one of the most common examples of any salon.

## 9. Strengthens Financial Health

- **Sustainability:** Prompt action can restore and stabilize your salon's financial health, ensuring that it continues to operate smoothly, grow, and scale. Regularly addressing any flaws or losses also ensures the sustainability of the business in the long term.

- **Profit Recovery:** By taking swift action to address financial flaws or losses, you create an opportunity to recover lost profits or restructure costs. The sooner you act, the sooner you can return to a profitable state.

## 10. Promotes Continuous Improvement

- **Ongoing Monitoring:** When you address financial flaws quickly, it encourages a habit of constant financial monitoring and improvement. It helps you stay proactive in managing finances rather than being reactive, and builds a culture of accountability and financial responsibility in your business.

# A Letter from the Author

*Dear Salonpreneur,*
First of all — thank you!

Thank you for choosing this book. Thank you for giving your time, your attention, and your heart to learn more about how to grow your salon business.
Over the past chapters, we've journeyed together through powerful insights — from managing staff and increasing client retention, to retailing smartly, handling difficult clients, leveraging AI, building strong vendor partnerships, and even expanding through franchising.

But reading alone is not enough.
**Now comes the real work — implementation.**

I truly believe that if you take even a few of the strategies and apply them in your daily salon routine, you will start seeing powerful results.

Your team will feel more aligned.
Your clients will keep coming back.
And yes — **your sales will double.**

Don't worry if you can't do everything at once. Big change starts with small, consistent steps. Trust yourself, trust the process, and take that first action today.

You've read the book.
Now live it. Apply it.
And if needed… read it again.

Your dream of running a successful salon isn't far away — it's just a few focused actions away.
Wishing you success, confidence, and lots of Happy Sales!

Warm regards,
**Gunjann Taneja**
*Author | Trainer | Salon Profit Expert*